D1450508

Comparative Social Policy
and the Third World

Studies in International Social Policy and Welfare

Edited by DR STEWART MacPHERSON, *Department of Social Administration, University of Nottingham, UK* and PROFESSOR JAMES MIDGLEY, *School of Social Work, Louisiana State University, USA*

This challenging series is designed to encourage the publication of books which deal with social policy issues in an international context. It will present new insights by highlighting the experience of different societies with regard to common problems. A major feature of the series will be its use of material from both non-industrial and industrial countries.

Titles in the series will be thematic in that they will explore current issues or theoretical propositions without relying exclusively on developments in any one country. Case studies of welfare programmes in particular countries will be avoided unless they are of special interest or draw conclusions of wider theoretical significance.

The series will make an important, innovative, contribution to the study of social policy by publishing books which make coherent, consistent use of international material for an international readership.

Forthcoming series titles:

The Welfare State in Capitalist Society
Ramesh Mishra

The Crisis in Welfare
Brian Munday (ed.)

Five Hundred Million Children
Stewart MacPherson

Modern Welfare States
Robert Friedmann, Neil Gilbert, Moshe Sherer (eds)

Comparative Social Policy and the Third World

Stewart MacPherson
Lecturer in Social Administration
University of Nottingham
and
James Midgley
Professor of Social Work
Louisiana State University

WHEATSHEAF BOOKS : SUSSEX

ST. MARTIN'S PRESS : NEW YORK

First published in Great Britain in 1987 by
WHEATSHEAF BOOKS LTD
A MEMBER OF THE HARVESTER PRESS PUBLISHING GROUP
Publisher: John Spiers
16 Ship Street, Brighton, Sussex
and in the USA by
ST. MARTIN'S PRESS, INC.
175 Fifth Avenue, New York, NY10010

© Stewart MacPherson and James Midgley, 1987

British Library Cataloguing in Publication Data
MacPherson, Stewart
    Comparative social policy and the Third World. —
    (Studies in international social policy and welfare; 1)
    1. Developing countries—Social policy
    I. Title   II. Midgley, James   III. Series
    361.6'1'091724   HN980

    ISBN 0–7450–0084–3

Library of Congress Cataloging-in-Publication Data
MacPherson, Stewart.
    Comparative Social Policy and the Third World.
    Bibliography: p.
    Includes index.
    1. Developing countries—Social policy.
    2. Social policy—Cross-cultural studies.
    I. Midgley, James.   II. Title.
    HN980.M264   1987   361.6'1'091724   87–4670
    ISBN 0–312–00851–1

Typeset in Times 11pt by Input Typesetting Ltd, London
Printed in Great Britain by Mackays of Chatham Ltd, Kent

THE HARVESTER PRESS PUBLISHING GROUP
The Harvester Group comprises Harvester Press Ltd (chiefly publishing
literature, fiction, philosophy, psychology, and science and trade books);
Harvester Press Microform Publications Ltd (publishing in microform
previously unpublished archives, scarce printed sources, and indexes to
these collections); Wheatsheaf Books Ltd (chiefly publishing in economics, international politics, sociology, women's studies and related social
sciences).

For
Andrea and Khadija

Contents

Tables

Preface

The intentions of this book are twofold. First, it offers a critique of the conventional methodology of comparative social policy research that treats cross-national enquiry as the documentation and analysis of welfare institutions in a handful of industrial countries. The bulk of comparative investigation in social policy has focused on Western Europe and North America, and particularly on Britain and the United States, making only occasional excursions into more distant territories. The critique of this convention calls for the extension of comparative social policy investigation to embrace many more societies of different cultural, economic and political characteristics. By expanding its narrow concerns, a broader and more veritable perspective in the subject can be promoted.

The book's second objective is to respond to this critique. By focusing attention on the two thirds of the world's nation states that are known collectively as the 'Third World' and which have been conspicuously neglected by comparative social policy investigators in the industrial countries, it seeks to contribute in a modest way to the emergence of a wider, comparative view. Although these societies are primarily engaged in agrarian productive activities and characterised by a high incidence of poverty and its associated social problems, they do have social development strategies, social policies and welfare programmes that are worthy of attention from comparative investigators. By discussing the social policies and welfare systems of these societies, this book seeks to extend the limited horizons of conventional social policy research and to facilitate the emergence of a global view in the subject.

The book has been written specifically for scholars and students of social policy in the industrial countries in order to inform them of developments in other parts of the world and to promote an awareness of the need for a world perspective. By examining the problems and issues of Third World social policy, it will also be of interest to those who are directly concerned with welfare matters in the developing countries. It will have interdisciplinary relevance to those in economics, sociology, political science and other subjects who are concerned with development problems. It is now more generally acknowledged that welfare considerations have been seriously neglected in development studies and that more attention needs to be paid to these issues. It is to be hoped that this book will begin to redress this omission.

In writing we have divided responsibility for the different topics between us: the authorship of chapters is attributed in the contents page.

Finally, this is the first in a new series sponsored by Wheatsheaf. Entitled *Studies in International Social Policy and Welfare* it will publish titles dealing with different social policy issues in a broad international context and, we hope, further promote the emergence of the global perspective advocated in this book.

Introduction: the Third World and comparative social policy

Systematic research into the social policies of governments is a comparatively new field of academic endeavour. Although philosophers, historians, social reformers and other commentators have written about social responses to social problems on many occasions in the past, it is only during the last few decades that studies of government intervention in meeting social needs and dealing with social problems have been carried out on a regular and systematic basis. Although these studies have examined many aspects of government social policy making, they have focused largely on policies governing the provision of health, social security, education, social work, housing and other social services.

Social policy research is pursued by scholars at universities located chiefly in the industrial countries. They include economists, political scientists and sociologists who have brought the different methodologies of their disciplines to bear on different facets of government social policy making. Although their work represents a minority interest in their academic fields, they have contributed significantly to the understanding of social welfare institutions in modern society. They have, for example, examined patterns of public expenditure on the social services, enquired into the administrative procedures adopted by governments to establish, deliver and ration the social services and analysed the functions these services have in society.

In addition to forming a specialist field within the major disciplines, social policy research is also undertaken on an interdisciplinary basis. This approach is probably best developed in Britain, where most universities have established academic departments of social administration which are wholly concerned with teaching and research in the field. Since the first of these departments were established in the 1950s, the interdisciplinary study of social administration at British universities has expanded rapidly and become an accepted field of academic endeavour. Although the current political climate in Britain is not conducive to the expansion of the subject, these departments continue to provide specialist expertise in the field.

The study of social policy has also become far more popular at schools of social work in the United States, which are the primary centres for welfare education and research in the country. Social policy is now regarded as an integral part of the social work curriculum at these schools, which were previously narrowly concerned with professional training, and it is given greater emphasis than ever before. There have been similar, although less formalised or extensive, developments at universities in other industrial countries. Although few Third World universities have established specialised departments of social administration, investigators at schools of social work and at disciplinary departments of economics, political science and sociology at these universities have initiated research into the social policies and programmes of their governments. This research is still limited in scope and largely dependent on ideas emanating from social policy investigators in Europe and North America, but a significant amount of knowledge about the social policies of developing countries has been accumulated. This enquiry has been aided by the research of a small number of investigators in the industrial countries who have taken a specialist interest in the field.

The growth of social policy as an academic subject was facilitated by the rapid expansion of statutory intervention in welfare matters by governments in the industrial nations during the middle decades of this century. The emergence of the so-called welfare state created a demand for trained personnel to staff the social services and for research into the social policies of governments. It was perhaps inevitable that the rise of welfarism as an ideology, the establishment of large social service bureaucracies and the allocation of substantial public resources to the social services should attract academic attention and facilitate the growth of systematic research into social policy and welfare programmes. This has resulted over the years in a rapid increase in the publication of books, journal articles and research reports into social policy issues and a refinement of the approaches and methodologies used by social policy investigators. The historico-descriptive method which characterised a good deal of social policy enquiry in previous years has been augmented by the more frequent application of theoretical perspectives for the analysis of social policy issues and the explanation of the origins, nature and functions of welfare institutions in modern societies.

The growing theoretical sophistication of social policy studies has been accompanied by a demand for comparative research. In their attempts to formulate broad generalisations and to conceptualise social policy issues in abstract terms, investigators have recognised the limitations of basing their research on the unique experiences of particular countries. Most are aware that social policy's claim to analytical significance can be strengthened by the construction of universal explanatory models. This realisation has stimulated more comparative social policy research and resulted in a somewhat broader appreciation of the welfare systems of other societies.

However, comparative analysis in social policy is still limited and largely cognisant of trends in a few industrial countries. Since the bulk of internationally disseminated social policy research is undertaken in the Western societies, this is perhaps not surprising. Apart from Britain and the United States, which feature prominently in the literature of comparative social policy, other favourites for comparative analysis include the Scandinavian countries (and Sweden in particular), France, West Germany and other European nations such as Austria and Italy, as well as more distant societies such as Australia, Canada, Israel and New Zealand. The Soviet Union is practically the only Communist country referred to by comparative social policy investigators. Initially, comparative social policy research sought to describe the essential features of the welfare programmes of two or more countries, pointing out the major similarities and differences between them. This case-study approach, as Madison (1980) revealed, has focused largely on social security and social work services. Examples include the pioneering 'constructive descriptions' by Rodgers *et al.* (1968, 1979), which compared a number of industrial countries, Heclo's (1974) account of the British and Swedish welfare systems and Rimlinger's (1971) study of the development of social policy in Europe, the United States and the Soviet Union. In addition to providing more specific country case studies for comparison, attempts have been made to abstract the findings of comparative research in general terms. Perhaps the best-known example of this approach is Higgins's (1981) examination of a variety of social policy issues which made reference to comparative developments in a number of industrial countries without providing detailed historico-descriptive narratives of the social services of particular societies. While this has resulted in the growing importance of comparative enquiry and its increasing relevance to social policy investigation, few would claim that comparative research in social policy has been properly integrated with the nationally focused enquiries of social policy researchers in the industrial nations. In spite of a greater knowledge of the social services and welfare systems of other countries, the study of social policy is still substantially dependent on the national perceptions of social policy investigators.

A major gap in comparative social policy is the neglect of those countries that are loosely categorised by Western social scientists as belonging to the Third World. These countries, which differ substantially in cultural, political and social characteristics, nevertheless share common distinguishing features that legitimate their differentiation from the Western industrial nations and the centrally planned societies of Eastern Europe. Among these features are certain economic, demographic and social characteristics that are widely believed to be related to a dependence on primary production, a colonial heritage and subordination to the demands of the world capitalist system. Although these societies comprise the majority of the world's nation states and contain more than two-thirds of the world's population, they are seldom referred to by comparative social policy investigators in the industrial countries. If it is true that comparative references to events in different industrial countries are neglected in social policy research, it may justifiably be argued that the Third World is ignored. Indeed, most social policy investigators in the West appear to be oblivious to the social policies and welfare programmes of the developing countries.

The neglect of the Third World is a reflection of the parochialism of many social policy researchers in industrial countries such as Britain and the United States who have often regarded their own societies as a macrocosm for social policy analysis. Although the discovery that other industrial countries also have complex welfare systems has broadened their horizons, it is nevertheless surprising that the Third World has remained distant from their experience, especially since political crises, mass poverty and disasters in the developing countries feature quite prominently in the news media. Since the seriousness of unmet social need in the developing countries affects humanity as a whole and requires concerted action at the global level, ignorance of the welfare problems of the Third World among Western social policy investigators would seem to be indefensible.

It would be wrong, however, to imply that no research has been undertaken into the social policies of the developing countries. Although Western scholars often assume that the study of Third World social policy is an underdeveloped field and that the neglect of the developing countries in comparative social policy is due to a paucity of research into the subject, this is an erroneous assumption. As this book will demonstrate, research into Third World social policy is today well developed. The literature covers a variety of issues and a large number of developing countries. Studies range in their complexity from those that are concerned with a particular welfare institution in one developing country to those that seek to provide a generalised account of the whole topic of Third World social policy. Although research into the social policies of the developing societies cannot be compared either in coverage or volume to the study of social policy in the West, a substantive and significant body of knowledge into Third World social policy now exists.

But the findings of this research are seldom related to the study of social policy in the West, and at present there exist two distinct worlds of comparative social policy enquiry dealing respectively with the industrial nations and the Third World. This compartmentalisation of comparative social policy research is, of course, a major impediment to the production of universal generalisations about welfare phenomena in the modern world. Although a number of interesting hypotheses have been formulated by social policy investigators, they have not been tested on a global scale. One example of this problem, as Jones (1983) pointed out, is the failure to examine the industrialisation-convergence hypothesis with reference to both the industrial and developing countries. This hypothesis posits that modern welfare institutions arise out of the industrial transformation of society. Because industrialisation weakens traditional responses to need, statutory provisions are required to maintain the needy and give social protection. Because a number of developing countries are experiencing a significant degree of industrial development, they offer an excellent opportunity to examine the usefulness of this theory in a large empirical field. But, as Jones observed, references to industrialisation and welfare in the developing countries are noticeably absent from the theoretical writings on the subject.

If social policy is to attain an acceptable level of theoretical significance, its propositions must be verified with reference to more societies outside Europe and North America. At present, comparative social policy is concerned either with the analysis of the welfare institutions of the industrial countries or, otherwise, with the study of social policy in the Third World. To promote the subject's analytical development, steps should be taken to integrate these two disparate worlds of social policy research to produce a global perspective that broadens social policy's focus and spans different communities and cultures and a multiplicity of economic, political and social situations. A global perspective would not only be cognisant of developments in welfare in different parts of the world but enable the formulation of concepts and theories that transcend specific issues in particular countries and regions to analyse those dimensions of social policy that can be comprehended in their generality.

Admittedly, there are formidable difficulties in promoting a global view of this kind. Apart from the perennial problems of inadequate data, there are theoretical and methodological obstacles to the realisation of this goal. As many researchers recognise, it is difficult enough to formulate valid propositions about welfare phenomena in one society—when a multiplicity of disparate political, social and economic settings are involved, the comprehension of this diversity and its encapsulation within a sustainable theoretical schema places severe cognitive demands on the investigator. The dynamic character of these phenomena may also limit the applicability of models for meaningful periods of time. There are serious difficulties also in comprehending and interpreting reality in other societies. Investigators who range over different cultures and nations in their search for generalities are at risk of misunderstanding events and of reaching conclusions that may fit their own conceptual proclivities but not the perceptions of the members of these societies. As ethnographic research has shown, the task of analysing just one culturally different community is faced with serious methodological difficulties which are compounded when several societies are compared.

In view of these problems, it may be argued that the cultural, political and economic heterogeneity of the modern world precludes the development of a global perspective in social policy and that quite different concepts and analytical insights are required when studying welfare phenomena in the societies of the Third World. Since the obstacles to the promotion of a truly comparative approach that integrates the two worlds of social policy research can be removed only with great difficulty, some may take the view that social policy analysis should be limited to domestic enquiry and the production of more modest propositions about particular societal events. However, this argument will have little appeal to social policy investigators seeking to foster the analytical sophistication of the subject. As has been argued already, the production of theoretical accounts that explain reality in truly general terms, requires a level of abstraction that encompasses different societal situations and transcends the domesticity of national enquiry.

The promotion of a global perspective in social policy should be encouraged because of the facts of a shrinking world system in which improvements in communications technologies, increased global power struggles and political interaction, greater world economic integration and mass tourism have heightened contact between different peoples. It is also compatible with developments in economics, sociology and political science, where scholars concerned with the study of Third World development have attempted to end the compartmentalisation of social science enquiry into the developing and industrial nations and sought to construct a unitary model for the analysis of the contemporary world system. The work of investigators such as Amin (1974, 1976), Emmanual (1974) and Wallerstein (1974, 1980) has facilitated a far broader conceptualisation of the social universe than that offered by conventional social science analysis. In their paradigm, particular societal realities are subsumed into an interactive global system in which, it is postulated, world capitalism determines national events and provides the dynamic momentum for future change. The explanatory insights of the world system theorists are not universally accepted by contemporary social scientists, nor have their accounts resulted in the integration of Third World research with that of the analysis of the industrial societies; but they have pioneered a new and more comprehensive approach in modern social science that has relevance for comparative social policy. The methodological insights of the world-systems theorists offer a framework for the analysis of world welfare problems and social policy responses which potentially encompasses the totality of the contemporary human condition.

The development of a global approach in social policy would also have useful normative consequences. The systematic study of social policy in a variety of societies and the integration of its findings can facilitate a better appreciation of the complexities of the social policy making process in different contexts and lead to the sharing of ideas and experiences. Although solutions to particular problems can best be found locally, the formulation of appropriate responses to social problems can be stimulated by a thorough knowledge of social experiments and welfare programmes adopted elsewhere. In this way, a more discerning exchange of experiences can be facilitated. As investigators such as MacPherson (1982) and Midgley (1981, 1984b) have shown, social policy making in the developing countries is still heavily dependent on inappropriate measures copied from the industrial countries, often during colonial times. A critical awareness of the diversity of social policy approaches in different situations can foster the emergence of confident, endogenous responses to social need.

There is another and more critical aspect to comparative social policy's normative relevance. As was noted previously, the pressing problems of mass poverty among the peoples of the developing world and the conditions of deprivation, oppression and exploitation under which they live has largely escaped comment from social policy investigators in the industrial nations. Preoccupied with issues of social service delivery, budgeting and administration in their own countries, they appear to be unaware of the problems of hunger, disease, ignorance, homelessness and landlessness which comprise the way of life for hundreds of millions of people in the Third World. The promotion of a global perspective in social policy would foster a greater concern for these problems and at the same time heighten awareness of the neglect of welfare considerations by the majority of governments in the industrial nations whose attitudes and policies towards the Third World are often governed by national interests and commercial advantage.

Contemporary international realities and developments in the social sciences suggest that the pursuit of a global perspective in social policy will enhance the subject, develop its theoretical potential and sharpen its normative relevance. While the difficulties and impediments to this type of enquiry must be recognised, efforts can be made to initiate the promotion of a wider and more internationally focused view of social policy issues. One step would be the dissemination of knowledge about social policy in the Third World. A better understanding of Third World issues among scholars not only in the industrial but in the developing nations would foster a proper appreciation of the welfare systems of other societies and broaden their horizons. Although researchers in Third World countries are knowledgeable about the welfare programmes of their own societies, they are often ignorant of events in other regions of the developing world. Although it may seem paradoxical, they are usually better informed about social policy in the industrial societies. One reason for this is their dependence on Western literature sources and limited publishing outlets for their own work. Also relevant is the perceived excellence of Western scholarship, which tends to foster the emulation of research models from the industrial world. The wider dissemination of knowledge about social policy in the developing countries and stimulation of more debates about social policy issues in the Third World can ease this dependence and simultaneously lessen the parochialism of much Western social policy research, contributing to a wider understanding of developments elsewhere. This, in turn, would help to promote the emergence of a global approach in which international developments in social policy are accorded as much significance as domestic events.

By examining various aspects of social policy in the Third World, this book seeks to make a modest contribution to the promotion of a global perspective in social policy studies. Its primary objective is to acquaint social policy investigators with the major welfare problems facing the developing countries and to review the emergence and present functioning of the social policies and social service programmes of these societies. It also endeavours to show how scholars concerned with the study of Third World social policy have approached the subject and how their studies may be classified and analysed.

Although this book seeks to provide a generalised account and to acquaint scholars with the field, it hopes to do more than enlighten and inform. It is the opinion of the authors that the analysis of welfare institutions in developing countries has direct relevance for social policy studies in other parts of the world, especially in the promotion and refinement of its analytical theories. As was noted earlier, explanatory theories of welfare have seldom been tested with reference to the developing countries. In an attempt to demonstrate the usefulness of this type of research, several theoretical propositions formulated by Western scholars are examined in the context of the Third World. Relevant research studies undertaken by scholars concerned with the study of social policy in the developing societies are reviewed to assess the global applicability of these theoretical approaches.

Another objective of the book is to examine the normative significance of Third World social policy studies both for the developing and industrial nations. It argues that a proper analysis of social policy in the developing countries can foster the formulation of appropriate measures that maximise welfare for ordinary people. Several examples are provided to show how inappropriate policy approaches may be modified and how imaginative and endogenous policy making may increase the relevance of social welfare programmes to the needs and circumstances of the developing societies. It is argued also that developments in Third World social policy have direct relevance to social policy making in the industrial countries. A good example is the relevance of the Third World's experience of community development to the trend towards greater decentralisation and people's participation in welfare in the industrial countries. The experience of community involvement in the Third World is extensive and has much to offer social planners and administrators seeking to develop similar programmes in the West.

To meet these various objectives, this book is divided into three parts. Part I provides a descriptive background to the subject, reviewing the nature and extent of social need and the development of welfare responses in Third World countries. Part II is concerned with the academic study of Third World social policy. It provides a broad review of the different approaches employed by social policy investigators concerned with Third World issues and examines the significance of this research for theoretical studies in the subject. Part III is concerned with the normative aspects of Third World social policy. It seeks to show how research in the field can inform policy makers in both the industrial and developing nations. Although there are other aspects of the study of Third World social policy that require comment and analysis, it is hoped that the topics dealt with in this book will stimulate more research and foster a greater appreciation of the relevance of Third World social policy studies for the development of a global perspective in the subject.

Part I
A Descriptive Prelude

1 Need and Deprivation in the Third World: A Profile

Most people in the industrial nations today are familiar with terms such as 'developing country' and 'Third World'. Media coverage of natural disasters, wars and famines has not only heightened awareness of the world's poorer countries but has linked these terms with vivid and enduring images of poverty and deprivation. However, these images are misleading. While the suffering they portray is real enough, the media's preoccupation with the sensational has facilitated the acceptance of a distorted definition of the Third World which conceals the very real economic and social progress that has been made in many developing countries during the postwar years.

Popular images of the Third World also conceal the heterogeneity of its constituent nation states. Although the developing countries have always been dissimilar in cultural, climatic, geographic and other characteristics, these differences have not been adequately recognised. Instead, social scientists have tended to stress the common features of these countries, and particularly their low levels of living and economic underdevelopment. But as a number of developing nations have experienced rapid economic growth and a significant degree of industrialisation, diversity rather than similarity has characterised the Third World. Today, many social scientists question the viability of the Third World construct, arguing that it is no longer possible to treat its constituent societies as a single group.

The increased differentiation of the developing nations has complicated the attempts of social policy investigators to formulate generalisations about social conditions in the Third World. Since different countries have experienced very different patterns of social development it is not surprising that the experts are divided in their assessments of whether there have been significant gains in levels of living in the Third World. Some countries have recorded marked improvements in incomes, health, education and other social conditions, while in others, progress has been minimal.

A profile of need in the developing world must, therefore, come to grips with the conceptual problems associated with the use of the 'Third World' construct. It must also deal with the problems of defining terms such as 'social need' in the context of underdevelopment. Both issues require some discussion and clarification before a review of welfare phenomena in the developing societies can be attempted.

THE THIRD WORLD: CONSTRUCT OR REALITY?

Although the practice of categorising peoples, cultures and societies is an ancient one, it is only in recent times that economic critera have been used for this purpose. Previously, political criteria were preferred, and these persisted even after the collapse of European imperialism, when, in spite of bitter struggles for national independence, the newly independent nation states maintained close links with their former colonial rulers. But as the conflicts of the Cold War intensified, these nations began to assert their autonomy, and the new geo-political concept of non-alignment gained currency. As a result, the world was increasingly seen as consisting of three major spheres, comprising the Western powers and their allies, the Soviet Union and its allies, and the non-aligned nations. Although the 'Third World' construct is generally thought to have emerged within the context of the struggle for non-alignment, it has no agreed derivation. Some authorities have argued that it was first used at the Bandung Conference of African and Asian non-aligned states in 1953. Others have claimed that it originated in France and that the notion of *Tiers Monde* was intended symbolically to parallel the *Tiers Etat* of the French revolution. Others have attributed the concept to Mao and his theory of the Three Worlds, which located the United States and the Soviet Union into the First World, the remaining industrial countries into the Second World and the poor, primary producing nations into the Third World.

The emergence of the economic emphasis in the Third World construct was facilitated by a growing realization that political independence required economic independence. Although the idea of economic development was hardly new, it became an important element in the emerging concept of statehood and was widely regarded as a mark of true sovereignty. The critique of neo-colonialism held that the new nation states could not claim to be free from world imperial influences until they had attained economic autarky. This argument was widely accepted in the 1950s and led numerous nationalist leaders to adopt industrialis-ation policies that were subsequently to prove disastrous for many countries. These ideas facilitated a fusion of geo-political and economic elements in the classification of the world's nation states and gave the 'Third World' concept its current meaning.

However, not everybody has been satisfied with the term, and there have been various attempts to replace it. Some have argued that it implies that the poorer nations are third class or that they comprise only a third of the world's coun-tries or a third of its population. *Less developed* and *under-developed* country were initially used, but they were super-ceded by the apparently more suitable *developing country* designation. However, during the 1970s, the term *under-developed* was resurrected by neo-Marxian writers of the dependency school and enjoyed some currency. Other terms which have been used include *poor, backward, industrial-ising* and *peripheral*, but these alternatives have not enjoyed great popularity. With the publication of the Brandt Report in 1981, the term *South* came into use and may in time prove to be acceptable.

More problematic than the choice of nomenclature, however, is the empirical validity of the 'Third World' construct. As has been suggested already, there is a growing recognition that the societies of the Third World are becoming more differentiated and dissimilar. Some authorities argue that momentous changes have taken place in the Third World during the last thirty or forty years and that the features of underdevelopment are no longer universally shared. Most noticeable has been the emergence of the so-called newly industrialising developing countries. Located largely in East Asia and Latin America, these countries have not only recorded high rates of economic growth but have undergone considerable industrialisation. At the same time, economic stagnation has characterised a number of developing countries, particularly in Africa. The differentiation of the Third World into the higher-income developing countries and the poorest 'Fourth World' countries has been compounded by increasing regional and sub-regional differences. These have often been associated with political conflicts and imperialist tensions as the world's two superpowers struggle to maintain and extend their spheres of influence. Attempts by the leaders of the non-aligned states to promote unity and to strengthen Third World solidarity have not been very successful.

In addition to the economic, social and political changes that have challenged the empirical validity of the Third World construct, there have been theoretical developments in the social sciences that have also called its viability into question. Differences of opinion about nomenclature have been accompanied by sharp disagreements about which nation states should be located into which categories. The emergence of world-systems theory (Amin, 1974, 1976; Wallerstein, 1974, 1980) has complicated matters further since it places little emphasis on sub-global categories and instead treats the world as a whole as a unit for analysis. Third World development is not regarded by these theorists as being separate from the development of the industrial countries. Similarly, Third World politics are treated as an integral part of world politics. The complex interactions, systems of reciprocity and patterns of complementarity that characterise the modern world are, these theorists believe, of far more analytical significance than the sub-global realities emphasised by those who use the 'Third World' construct.

While these empirical changes and theoretical objections suggest that the Third World category has serious limitations and should be abandoned, it would be premature to do so now. In spite of its weaknesses, the 'Third World' construct retains heuristic value and an essential validity. The common elements of a colonial heritage, a susceptibility to imperial manipulation, a dependence on primary commodities and a vulnerability to the vagaries of world markets are just some of the common features that characterise the world's poorer nations, including many that have experienced industrialisation. These similarities are even more marked when welfare criteria are employed. As will be shown in this chapter, high rates of economic growth are no antidote to poverty. With the exception of very few developing countries, and in spite of significant social progress during the last three decades, the problem of mass poverty remains a valid common denominator and the most compelling argument for the continued use of the 'Third World' construct.

Nevertheless, the facts of differentiation and heterogeneity must be recognised, as must the analytical insights of the world-systems theorists. Both will be taken into account in the subsequent discussion where the 'Third World' construct will be used in a general rather than rigorous way, and where cultural, regional, economic, political and other differences will be constantly emphasized.

THE CONCEPTUALIZATION OF NEED

Although the concept of need is of fundamental importance in social policy research, it is still vaguely formulated. As Bradshaw's (1972) widely cited analysis revealed, 'need' may be defined in different ways. The term has various meanings, and it is not always clear which elements social policy investigators are emphasising when they use it. There are disagreements also about whether the concept refers to objective states which have intrinsic qualities that elicit particular responses or whether needs are conditions that are designated through the political process as requiring these responses. There are disagreements also about whether social needs can be distinguished from demands. Although conventional social policy analysis has implied that needs are different from demands in that they have inherent characteristics that facilitate the expression of altruistic feelings, there have been differences of opinion on this question.

While it is not possible to examine these arguments here in any detail, the limitations of the concept of need should be recognised. This is particularly important in the context of Third World social policy studies, where research into social needs is still underdeveloped. Nevertheless, there have been various attempts to formulate a conceptual basis for Third World social policy enquiry around a common concept of social need, and these have been of some value in facilitating a better understanding of the nature of the social problems facing the developing countries.

One of the first attempts to define and measure social need in the Third World context arose out of the efforts of the United Nations to promote social planning in the developing countries. Concerned about the obsession with economic growth in development circles, the United Nations began in the late 1960s to encourage its Third World member states to adopt social planning procedures in their planning ministries (Midgley, 1984e). A key element in this approach was the recognition that social indicators would be needed to measure and monitor social progress. Although the United Nations had been interested in social welfare measurement for many years, publishing one of the first documents on the subject as long ago as 1954, it was the involvement of the United Nations Research Institute for Social Development (UNRISD) in Geneva, and particularly the contributions of Drewnowski (1970) and MacGranahan (1970), that fostered the levels of living conceptualization of need.

Baster (1972, 1985) has summarised this work in detail, showing that Drewnowski and MacGranahans's approaches shared many common features. Basic to their methodologies was the collection of an extensive array of separate social, economic and political measures that were amalgamated into a unitary index of social development. This index was then applied to measure levels of living in different countries or regions for which data were available.

This research attracted widespread attention and encouraged the formulation of various similar welfare indices. Perhaps the best known is Morris's (1979) Physical Quality of Life Index (PQLI), which is based on three common measures—life expectancy, infant mortality and literacy. Using the PQLI, Morris was able to assess the extent of social need in a large number of countries. A more recent and comprehensive levels-of-living measure is Estes's Index of Social Progress (ISP), which was designed to measure 'differential levels of human deprivation and suffering experienced by people living anywhere in the world' (Estes, 1984: 17). Comprised of forty-four welfare-related social indicators, Estes applied the ISP to examine the extent and nature of social need on a global scale during the 1970s and early 1980s. Unlike the PQLI, which is scored on a continuum of zero to 100 units, the ISP scores related to a constant of 100 units, which is the ISP score for all countries regions and continents.

A different approach to the conceptualization and measurement of social need in the Third World emerged from research undertaken into unemployment and underemployment by the International Labour Office (ILO) in the early 1970s. Various ILO studies concluded that the employment problems facing the developing countries were not a consequence of ineffective labour utilisation as had been supposed but were a manifestation of poverty. Attempts to create remunerative employment could not, therefore, be separated from the wider issue of eradicating poverty. In 1976, at the World Employment Conference, the ILO unveiled its new Basic Needs approach to development, which called on the governments of developing countries to take direct action to improve the health, education and nutritional status of their citizens and to provide clean drinking water and sanitary facilities (Streeten *et al*, 1981).

The identification of social need with central welfare

concerns such as health, education and nutrition was a somewhat different approach to that used by the levels-of-living investigators. It linked the concept of need directly to the provision of public services (in a way that will be familiar to students of Western social policy) and introduced a sectoral element into the debate, differentiating between various types of social needs and associated fields of service delivery.

These two methodological approaches towards the analysis of social need in the Third World will be used together with other data and measures in the remainder of this chapter. However, both approaches have drawbacks and should be regarded as offering no more than general guidelines for analysis. In the subsequent account, an attempt will be made first to examine social needs in terms of quantitative measures such as income data and indicators. Second, the social situation will be discussed with reference to major fields of service provision such as health, education and housing. In both approaches, regional and other variations will be emphasised and an effort will be made to examine trends over time. But first, to place the discussion in a wider context, a brief examination of the Third World's demographic situation, economic trends and political realities will be attempted.

THE DEMOGRAPHIC, ECONOMIC AND POLITICAL CONTEXT

Although various estimates of the world's population have been made, most experts believe that there were more than 4,000 million people on earth at the beginning of the 1980s—some estimates suggest a figure approaching 4,500 million (United Nations, 1980). Most believe that the population of the Third World amounts to between two-thirds to three-quarters of the world's total population. If the Third World is defined as including all the countries of Africa, Asia (except Japan) and Central and South America, this figure was about 74 per cent in 1980 (Loup, 1983).

Table 1.1 provides information about the distribution of

the world's population. As may be seen from the table, Asia contains the largest portion of the world's and the Third World's population. The region also contains the two most populous countries on earth—China (1,008 million) and India (717 million)—as well as three other countries which rank among the Third World's most heavily populated nations: these are Indonesia (152 million), Bangladesh (92 million) and Pakistan (87 million). Asia also has the highest population densities in the Third World, well above those of Africa and Central and South America. With the exception of countries like Nigeria (91 million), Brazil (126 million) and Mexico (73 million), the African and Central and South American regions are comparatively less populated; indeed, a number of countries with sizeable territories such as Botswana, Namibia, Guyana and Surinam have populations of less than a million people.

Table 1.1: *Distribution of the world's population*

Region	Population 1950 millions	%	Population 1980 millions	%	Density (person/sq. km) 1950	1980
Africa	219	8.7	467	10.6	7.2	15.4
Asia	1,298	51.7	2,447	55.4	47.0	88.6
Central and South America	164	6.5	368	8.4	8.0	17.9
Third World	1,681	66.9	3,284	74.4	21.0	41.8
Industrial countries	832	33.1	1,131	25.6	14.5	19.7
World	2,513	100.0	4,415	100.0	18.5	32.5

Sources: Loup (1983), United Nations (1984).

Information about population growth in the Third World is provided in Table 1.2. Between 1950 and 1980 the world's population increased by about 75 per cent. While the population of the industrial countries increased by 35 per cent, the population of the Third World almost doubled.

The rapid increase in the Third World's population is usually attributed to a sharp decline in mortality accompanied by sustained or only slightly declining fertility. It is generally

Table 1.2 *World population increase, 1950–80*

Region	Population increase 1950–80 millions	%	Average annual crude birth rate per 1,000	Average annual natural increase rate %
Africa	250	114	46.0	2.8
Asia	1,149	88	30.3	1.9
Central and South America	204	124	35.4	2.7
Third World	1,603	95	33.6	2.0
Industrial countries	299	35	15.6	0.6
World	1,902	75	28.9	1.7

Source: Loup (1983).

accepted that improvements in health, nutrition, sanitation and associated environmental factors have contributed significantly to reductions in mortality. But, with low mortality and high fertility, the rates of natural population increase recorded in many developing countries have been exceptionally rapid, and it is only in recent years that declines in natural increase have been recorded. For the developing countries as a whole, natural increase has fallen from a peak of about 2.4 per cent in the 1960s to about 2 per cent in the 1980s. The major exception is sub-Saharan Africa, where natural increase has risen steadily since 1950. A very slight decline has been recorded in the Middle East and in North Africa, but more significant falls have taken place in East Asia and especially in China. Indeed, China's rapidly declining natural increase rate is a major factor in the gradual decline in natural increase in the Third World as a whole. Generally, these declines in natural increase rates are due to falls in fertility. In China, for example, the total fertility rate fell by 61 per cent between 1965 and 1980. Falling natural increase rates in other East Asian countries such as Korea and Thailand are also due to a reduction in fertility. Natural increase rates for different regions of the Third World for the period 1950 to 1980 are shown in Table 1.3.

Table 1.3: *Natural increase rates in different Third World regions,*
1950–80

Region	1950 (%)	1965 (%)	1980 (%)
Africa and Middle East	2.5	2.8	2.7
South Asia	2.1	2.7	3.1
East Asia	1.7	2.5	2.2
China	2.6	2.7	1.1
Central and South America	2.6	2.8	2.5

Source: World Bank (1984).

In spite of these declines, population growth in the Third
World, and especially in the African region, remains high.
In sub-Saharan Africa, where natural increase is about 3
per cent per annum, the population will double in less than
nine years (World Bank, 1984). Also, indications of a falling
rate of natural increase in some regions does not mean that
population size will decline, or even that it will remain
static. Because most developing countries have very young
populations, often with more than 40 per cent aged 15 years
or less, sustained growth in absolute population numbers
may be expected for the foreseeable future.

In the Third World, the spatial aspect of the demographic
situation is characterised by a concentration of the population in rural areas, by migration towards the urban areas
and by rapid urban growth rates. Table 1.4 shows that
although the majority of the Third World's population
continues to live in the countryside, the proportion has
dropped steadily from about 83 per cent in 1950 to about
70 per cent in 1980. However, it should be stressed that
these declines refer to proportions and do not imply that the
size of the rural population has fallen. In most developing
countries, rural populations continue to grow rapidly, albeit
it at a somewhat slower rate than urban populations.

The changing distribution of the proportions of the populations living in urban and rural areas in the developing
countries is due both to migration from the countryside and
to high rates of natural population increase in the cities. In
spite of their sprawling shanty towns and visible manifestations of poverty and squalor, many Third World cities

Table 1.4: *Urban–rural distribution, 1950–80*

Region	1950 urban (%)	1950 rural (%)	1980ᵉ urban (%)	1980ᵉ rural (%)
Africa	14.5	85.5	28.9	71.1
Asia	16.2	83.8	27.9	72.1
Central and South America	41.2	58.8	64.7	35.3
Third World	16.7	83.3	30.5	69.5
Industrial countries	52.4	47.6	71.2	29.8
World	28.9	71.1	41.3	58.7

e = estimate.
Source: Todaro (1979).

have lower mortality rates than the rural areas, and because of high urban fertility rates, their populations have grown rapidly. This growth has been augmented by a steady flow of rural migrants to the cities. Average annual urban growth rates for different Third World regions are shown in Table 1.5. As this table reveals, Africa's urban growth is exceptionally high reflecting the contribution of both migration and natural population increase to the growth of the region's cities.

Table 1.5: *Average annual urban growth rates, 1950–80*

Region	1950–60 (%)	1975–80 (%)	1980–90ᵉ (%)
Africa	4.4	5.1	5.0
Asia	4.5	3.6	3.6
Central and South America	4.5	3.7	3.5
Third World	4.5	4.1	4.0
Industrial countries	2.4	1.6	1.5
World	3.3	2.9	2.9

e = estimate.
Source: Todaro (1979).

Economic Trends
Very little information about economic growth in the developing countries before the Second World War is available. As Morawetz (1977) observed, early postwar concerns

with the economic problems of the 'foreign areas' concentrated largely on the reconstruction of Germany and Japan rather than the economic underdevelopment of the colonial world. Consequently, most estimates of economic growth rates in the Third World before 1950 are speculative. Nevertheless, Bairoch (1975) calculated that the growth of per capita GDP between 1900 and 1950 in the developing countries averaged less than 1 per cent (0.8%) per annum and that overall GDP increases averaged about 2 per cent.

During the 1950s, overall economic growth rates as well as per capita income began to improve. Table 1.6 provides information about per capita incomes and average annual growth rates during the period 1950 to 1980. Similar data for countries of different levels of development for 1960 to 1980 are provided in Table 1.7. It should be stressed, however, that these figures are no more than approximations since data are not available for a number of countries. Also, the per capita income for Asia is artificially high since it includes the region's oil exporting nations. If they are excluded, the region's per capita income is only 1,012 dollars and even this figure is inflated by the performance of the newly industrialising countries of East Asia. Nevertheless, the table does show underlying trends and patterns.

Most economists accept that per capita economic growth in the developing countries as a whole has been impressive.

Table 1.6: *Per capita incomes and growth rates by regions, 1950–80*

Region	Per capita income		Average annual growth rate	
	1950 (US $)	1980 (US $)	1950–60 (%)	1960–80 (%)
Africa	170	754	2.4	1.3
Asia	225	1,012[a]	3.3	3.5
Central and South America	495	1,605	2.5	2.3
Third World	296	3,157	2.7	2.5
Industrial Countries[b]	1,449	10,330	4.4	3.6

a = excludes Asian oil exporting countries.
b = excludes European communist countries.
Sources: Morawetz (1977), World Bank (1982).

Table 1.7: *Per capita incomes and growth rates by level of development,
1960–80*

Category	Per capita income 1980 (US $)	Average annual growth rate 1960–80 (%)
Low-income developing countries	260	1.2
Middle-income developing countries	1,400	3.8
High-income oil exporters	12,320	6.3
Industrial countries[a]	10,320	3.6

a = excludes European communist countries.
Source: World Bank (1984).

During the 1950s and 1960s, all regions of the Third World
recorded high rates of GDP growth, and in spite of a simultaneously high rate of population growth, per capita
incomes rose steadily. Highest rates during this period were
recorded in Central and South America, but African and
Asian rates were also well above those expected by many
economists. Because the industrial countries had recorded
per capita income increases of no more than 2 per cent per
annum during the period of their most rapid industrialisation, the high per capita growth rates observed in the
developing countries in the 1950s and 1960s surprised most
economic forecasters. Even at the beginning of the First
United Nations Development Decade in 1960, many were
pessimistic about the economic prospects of the Third
World. Surveying some sixty-six developing countries,
Rosenstein-Rodan (1961) took the view that growth rates
of 3 per cent or more were unlikely. But, as Loup (1983)
pointed out some twenty years later, eighteen countries
exceeded this figure. Some, such as Korea and Singapore,
which Rosenstein-Rodan believed had limited prospects,
had rates well in excess of 3 per cent.

It must be recognised, however, that these overall trends
mask significant differences between the developing countries as well as variations in performance between the major
economic sectors. Within the different regions, some countries recorded relatively low rates of growth. In others,
where growth rates were higher, these were often due to

increased exports of minerals or rises in mineral prices rather than a significant change in the economy. Also, rapid economic growth was often confined to the small urban sector which had been created during the colonial era, and generally it was the expansion of this sector that characterized the impressive performance of most developing countries. The bulk of the population remained dependent on subsistence agriculture or cash cropping for their livelihood.

On the other hand, a number of developing countries, located chiefly in South America and East Asia, experienced significant changes. In these countries, substantial investments in industry began to gradually transform their economies, creating stable wage employment, significant improvements in levels of living and the conditions for sustained long-term development. In other countries, industrialisation lagged, and with increasing economic problems during the 1970s and 1980s, growth rates slowed dramatically. In some regions, and especially in sub-Saharan Africa, the neglect of agriculture resulted in a decline in agricultural production. With increasing population growth, per capita agricultural output and food availability fell creating serious problems.

Industrial development in some countries and economic stagnation in others has produced markedly divergent development trends in the Third World. The poorer, primary agricultural producers of sub-Saharan Africa and South Asia have become more differentiated from the newly industrialising countries of South America and East Asia. Cooperation between the oil exporting developing countries in the 1970s, which brought about a substantial increase in the prices of petroleum products, further heightened these differences. Sharp rises in energy costs in the 1970s have also had a profound effect on the world's economy, exacerbating many of the problems which had already begun to manifest themselves in the late 1960s. Inflation, currency instability and a rapid rise in the prices of raw materials were already causing serious problems in the industrial countries, and these were aggravated by the oil crisis. With recession in the West, many Third World nations suffered serious economic setbacks during the 1970s and 1980s.

During this period, a number of developing countries recorded negative rates of per capita economic growth, and in some, such as Angola, Iran, Iraq, Lebanon and Kampuchea, violent conflicts have caused serious economic disruption. Faced with rising energy costs and falling exports, many developing countries increased their dependency on external financing. This trend continued during the decade, resulting in a high level of indebtedness. During the 1970s, for example, the Third World's debt level increased from US $87 billion to $525 billion, and by 1984 had reached $592 billion dollars. Debt service has risen substantially, and for the developing countries as a whole it amounted to about 12 per cent of exports at the end of the 1970s and about 20 per cent by 1983 (World Bank, 1984). Information on Third World debt is shown in Table 1.8. The debt problem is not only a major impediment to the economic recovery of the developing countries but is also a matter of concern to the industrial nations as well.

Table 1.8: *Third World indebtedness, 1984*

Category	Outstanding debt (US $, billions)	% of GNP	Debt service as % of exports
Low-income developing countries	69.7	25.4	17.4
Middle-income developing countries	522.3	35.0	23.3
All developing countries	592.0	26.7	20.5

Source: World Bank (1984).

At present, the economic prospects for the developing countries are decidedly mixed. The debt problem, the world recession and sluggish demand for primary commodities are just some of the problems they face. Although these factors pose a far more serious threat to the poorest countries, the higher-income developing countries have also been affected. Nevertheless, it is the poorest countries that are the most vulnerable. As the Ethiopian famine of 1984–85 revealed, millions of people in the Third World live a precarious existence in which the struggle for survival can quickly be defeated, producing human suffering on an awful scale.

Political Realities

The postwar division of the world's nation states into 'Eastern' and 'Western' spheres of influence did not, as many predicted, produce an enduring geo-political situation. The non-aligned nations emerged to create a third force in world politics which, while not seeking to compete with the two superpowers, refused to take sides. Since then, however, shifting allegiances, changes in governments and the efforts of the superpowers to extend their influence have further complicated the situation, rendering the threefold geo-political division obsolete.

The increasing complexity of international political alignments has been accompanied by equally complex developments at the regional level. Marxist governments have come to power in regions that were once thought to be the preserve of the Western powers. But this has not always resulted in a close association between these governments and the Eastern communist states. Indeed, a number of African Marxist governments maintain close links with their former colonial rulers. This does not suggest, however, that global imperial struggles are over. American involvement in Central America and Soviet intervention in Afghanistan demonstrate that imperialism remains a major world force. Nor indeed, have the former colonial powers ceased to engage in military expeditions to preserve their interests; both Britain and France have done so in recent years. Although direct superpower intervention is now more limited, international military conflicts are still common. Estes (1984) reported that some forty-five nations were engaged in 'wars' of one kind or another in the early 1980s; some of these have lasted for as long as ten years, killing between 5 million and 10 million people.

At the national level there has been a continued trend towards authoritarianism and the militarisation of government. Although most developing countries inherited parliamentary democratic constitutions from their former colonial rulers, many have become one-party states, and dictatorship is common. Often the dictators are military officers. Estes (1984) found that almost two-thirds of the countries he surveyed had military or quasi-military governments in 1983; in 1970 only a third had military governments. The trend towards the militarisation of politics in the Third World has been associated with rapid increases in military expenditures. The Brandt Report (Brandt *et al.*, 1980) revealed that world military spending was approaching $450 billion a year while world aid flows amounted to only $20 billion a year; 70 per cent of all military exports go to the developing countries. Table 1.9 provides information about military and social expenditure in different groups of countries. Of interest is the comparatively large proportion of the national budget devoted to military expenditures in both the poorest developing nations and the richest oil exporters. With the exception of the Western industrial countries, health expenditures are significantly lower than military allocations. No information for Eastern Europe is available.

Table 1.9: *Military and social expenditures as percentages of total public expenditures*

Category	Military	Education	Health
Low-income developing	18.3	5.9	2.9
Middle-income developing country	9.6	14.3	5.3
High-income oil exporters	28.0	9.2	5.5
Industrial countries[a]	13.6	5.1	11.4

a = excludes European communist countries.
Source: World Bank (1984).

Political authoritarianism in many developing countries has been accompanied by an increase in human rights violations. Although these violations also occur in the industrial countries, some Third World governments now systematically contravene human rights. Detention and execution without trial, restrictions on travel and officially sanctioned torture, often with the connivance of medical professionals, is institutionalised in a number of countries. Similarly, blatant discrimination on the basis of gender, religious belief, ethnicity and political opinion is widespread. Child labour is common in many developing countries, debt bondage still frequently occurs in South Asia, and slavery is still found in parts of Africa.

SOCIAL NEED AND UNDERDEVELOPMENT

Prevailing demographic, economic and political conditions in the developing countries are closely related to the social problems that concern social policy investigators. Economic underdevelopment, a large rural population, a dependence on agricultural production and rapid demographic increases are directly associated with a high incidence of absolute poverty, low standards of health and education, poor shelter and various other social ills. The social problems of under-development are also related to the political realities of the Third World. In many developing countries, dictatorship, military totalitarianism and other forms of concentrated political power have exacerbated adverse social conditions.

Although demographic, economic and political factors are relevant to an understanding of the nature of social need in the Third World today, they do not provide adequate information about levels of living and poverty, or about health, education or housing. For this reason, this section of the chapter is concerned with the particular forms of social need that have been the conventional focus of the social services. In addition, it examines the extent to which social conditions in the Third World have improved or deteriorated over recent decades. As indicated at the beginning of this chapter, there have been very significant gains in welfare in many developing countries. Nevertheless, performance has been very uneven. While many Third World countries have experienced real improvements in levels of living, some others have not.

There have also been variations in performance between the different social sectors. Generally, while educational enrolments and literacy rates have improved considerably in most parts of the Third World, housing conditions remain very unsatisfactory, even in many middle-income developing countries. As suggested previously, the hetero-geneity of the developing countries and their divergent experience of social development complicates the situation and confounds the attempts of social scientists to provide simple answers to questions about social progress in the Third World. For these reasons, comments about improvements in social conditions in this chapter will be related to specific social welfare concerns and to trends in different regions of the Third World.

Poverty and Levels of Living
One major social welfare concern is poverty and levels of living. As shown earlier, the levels-of-living approach to the study of social need in the Third World has produced a number of useful welfare indices which amalgamate separate social indicators to provide general insights into social conditions. Table 1.10 summarises the scores of two indices of this type; they are Morris's (1979) PQLI and Estes's (1984) ISP. As will be remembered, the PQLI is scored between zero and 100 units, while ISP scores relate to a global index of 100 units.

Table 1.10: *Levels-of-living index scores, PQLI and ISP*

Region	PQLI (n = 74)	ISP (n = 107)
Africa	28.3	51.9
Asia	63.2	104.6
Central and South America	74.9	113.3
Third World	55.5	89.9
Industrial countries	83.0	151.5

Sources: Morris (1979), Estes (1984).

Because the two indices are based on different component measures and provide information for different countries at different periods of time, they are not directly comparable. Nevertheless, they do reveal remarkably similar trends. As may be seen from Table 1.10, African countries had the lowest scores on both indices, while those in Central and South America were the highest. Both Morris and Estes reported significant shifts in their respective index scores over time. But while the PQLI showed steady improvements in all regions from the 1950s to the 1970s, the ISP recorded a negative shift for African countries of nearly 10 per cent during the 1970s and only a small gain of 1.2 per cent for Central and South America. The ISP gain for Asia was somewhat more significant, showing a 8.2 per cent increase during the decade. For Africa, the ISP sub-indices revealed significant losses on economic indicators as well as the key social indicators. These findings are in keeping with the evidence produced earlier: not only are the African countries among the poorest in the world but their development record in the last fifteen years has been very uneven.

Although these indices provide useful information about levels of living in different parts of the world and overcome many of the methodological problems associated with the use of poverty lines, they do not adequately describe the poverty problem in the Third World in a way that is readily comprehended. For this reason, many social scientists believe that in spite of its drawbacks, the poverty line approach, with its attempt to quantify the incidence of poverty, offers the most useful insights.

Although poverty lines have been used in the developing countries for many years, it is only in comparatively recent times that they have been employed to make estimates of the incidence of poverty on a global scale. Research undertaken by Ahluwalia (1974) at the World Bank pioneered this approach, showing that some 370 million people in forty-four countries, for which information was available, had incomes below an absolute poverty line of $50 in 1969; altogether 580 million had incomes below the $75 line. Ahluwalia made a number of generalisations that were subsequently confirmed. First, he observed that poverty is concentrated in the most economically underdeveloped countries, and particularly in sub-Saharan Africa and South Asia. However, absolute poverty also occurred in countries with comparatively high incomes. For example, Ecuador, with a per capita income three times as high as that of Sri Lanka, had about the same incidence of poverty. Both economic development and income distribution, Ahluwalia concluded, were relevant factors in the aetiology of poverty.

Ahluwalia's pioneering research paved the way for more

comprehensive estimates of the incidence of absolute poverty in the Third World. In a speech to the Governors of the World Bank in 1973, the Bank's president, Robert MacNamara, stated that the number of people in absolute poverty in the world as a whole amounted to about 800 million; this estimate was based on Ahluwalia's research. Another estimate which was also based on Ahluwalia's investigations, came from the International Labour Office in 1976. This estimate differentiated between the 'destitute', who numbered about 706 million, and the 'seriously poor', who comprised another 500 million. Although various other estimates (including a revised figure by Ahluwalia and his associates) have also been published, most suggest a figure of between 500 and 700 million for various dates in the 1970s. The major exception is Hopkins (1980), who put the figure well above 1,000 million. These various estimates are shown in Table 1.11.

Table 1.11: *Estimates of the incidence of absolute poverty*

Estimator	Number in poverty (millions)	Year
Ahluwalia (1974)	370 ($50)	1969
	580 ($75)	1969
MacNamara (1973)	800	1973
ILO (1976)	706 (destitute)	
	500 (seriously poor)	1972
World Bank (1975)	560	1969
Ahluwalia *et al.* (1978)	770	1975
Hopkins (1980)	1,102	1974
Fields (1981)	800	1970

Various estimates of the incidence of absolute poverty in the different regions of the Third World are available. Table 1.12 is based on forecasts made by Hopkins (1982). Although his estimates are higher than most others, his figure of 1,144 million is a realistic one. Like most other investigators, Hopkins concluded that the majority of the world's poor live in Asia and particularly in South Asia. Indeed, an earlier World Bank (1975) report estimated that almost two-thirds of the world's poor live in just four countries in the region: Bangladesh, India, Indonesia and Pakistan. But it should be remembered that the concentration of poverty in this region is also a function of its large population size. While Africa, with a much smaller population, contained a relatively small proportion of the world's poor, the incidence of poverty within the region was almost as high as in Asia.

Table 1.12: *Estimated incidence of poverty in different world regions, 1982*

Region	Number (millions)	% of regional total	% of world total
Africa	200	53	17.9
Asia	788	60	70.7
Middle East	36	18	3.2
Central and South America	86	24	7.7
Industrial countries	4	3	.5
World total	1,114	47	100.0

Source: Hopkins (1982).

Within countries, poverty is particularly characteristic of the agricultural sector. Although it is often assumed that cities have far more poverty than rural areas, this is an erroneous assumption based on perceptions of highly visible manifestations of urban squalor and poor housing. Lipton (1977) reviewed survey data for a number of developing countries, showing that urban incomes are considerably higher than rural incomes. Although the towns do have poor people, the majority of the poor are found in the countryside. Levels-of-living indicators show similar urban–rural differentials, and generally, rural areas have more restricted access to modern social services (Hardiman and Midgley, 1982b). The rural areas also contain the very poorest groups in the Third World. Landless labourers, nomads, shifting cultivators and hunter-gatherers who often live in remote areas are in desperate poverty and have levels of living which are far below those of city dwellers as well as those of average agricultural households.

It must be remembered that these estimates of poverty are based on near-starvation poverty lines and that the data do not portray the qualitative aspects of deprivation that characterise the lives of between 40 per cent and a half of the world's population. Obviously, figures can never convey the desperate conditions of hunger, ill-health, illiteracy and inadequate housing under which the poor subsist. Nor do they provide information about the situation of the poor in comparison with the minority of the Third World's population who have an exceptionally high standard of living. This privileged group of political élites, businessmen, executives, landowners, civil servants, military officers and professionals enjoy a level of living that equals and sometimes surpasses that of their counterparts in the industrial world. Their privileges cannot be separated from the poverty which afflicts the rest of the population. As suggested earlier, poverty and inequality are inextricably linked.

Inequality
Although the issue is controversial, a substantial number of development experts today believe that the poverty problem in the Third World is closely related to inequality. Although many developing countries have experienced good rates of economic growth, the benefits of growth have not been widely distributed among the population, and instead only a small privileged minority have benefited. This accounts for the fact that a number of developing countries (such as Ecuador, which was mentioned previously) with high per capita incomes have a comparatively high incidence of absolute poverty. Although inequality was originally thought to be a separate issue and quite unrelated to the task of maximising economic growth, it is now much more widely accepted in development circles that attempts to reduce poverty must deal simultaneously with the concentration of income and wealth in the Third World.

There is a good deal of evidence to show that income inequalities in the developing countries are particularly marked. In a pioneering study, Kuznets (1955) found that the pattern of income distribution in the Third World was much more unequal than in the Western industrial countries. In a later study which reviewed data for a larger number of countries, Kuznets (1963) confirmed this finding.

Numerous other investigators, including Kravis (1960), Oshima (1962), Adelman and Morris (1973) and Ahluwalia (1974), agreed with Kuznet's conclusion. Ahluwalia's research, which was the most comprehensive at the time, concluded that the poorest 40 per cent of the population in the developing countries received, on average, only 12.5 per cent of income. In the industrial countries, on the other hand, the poorest 40 per cent received some 20 per cent of income. In twenty-three of the developing countries for which data were available, the poorest 40 per cent received only 9 per cent of income.

Attention has also focused on the question of whether patterns of inequality in the Third World change with economic development. Kuznets (1955) was one of the first to examine this issue, suggesting that income inequality worsens in the early stages of development but then becomes less marked as development proceeds. Explaining this finding, Kuznets argued that increased inequality during the early stages of development could be attributed to the higher incomes earned by those who enter the expanding modern sector of the economy. As the economy absorbs more labour, larger numbers of people benefit and inequality declines.

Kuznets's finding has been widely accepted and has even been quoted by some writers to rationalise inequalities in the Third World. Numerous investigators have also confirmed his conclusions, and in one account, which extended on his ideas, Adelman and Morris (1973) claimed that a worsening of inequality is accompanied by an absolute fall in the living standards of the poorest groups. Although this finding was not universally accepted, it was widely cited. While there is evidence to show that the lowest income groups in some developing countries in South Asia and sub-Saharan Africa have been impoverished as a consequence of economic stagnation, population growth and entrenched inequality, there is little evidence to show that the phenomenon is a universal feature of the development experience. Indeed, a careful examination of the data by Ahluwalia

(1976) questioned the whole basis of this conclusion. Noting that most studies of income inequality over time are based on cross-sectional data, Ahluwalia revealed that time-series data do not support either Kuznets or Adelman and Morris's findings.

Nevertheless, the facts of inequality in the Third World are indisputable. Particularly vivid are the feudal practices of sharecropping and debt bondage, which reduce hundreds of millions of people to a life of servitude. These institutions are not only morally abhorrent but effectively impede the development efforts of the Third World. Land concentration and primitive feudal practices suppress incentives and perpetuate agricultural stagnation. By failing to deal with these practices, the governments of many Third World countries have contributed to economic backwardness and the maintenance of low levels of living among the mass of the population.

Disease and Ill-Health

It is today more widely accepted that health and social conditions are interrelated and that the problem of ill-health in the Third World cannot be aetiologically separated from the poverty problem. Many millions of people in the developing countries die or are debilitated by diseases which are closely associated with poverty. Communicable diseases such as tuberculosis, malaria and infectious diarrhoea, which are rife in the Third World, have practically disappeared from the industrial countries, not because of new medical technologies but because of significant improvements in levels of living.

Although the links between disease and social conditions in the Third World are now better understood, statistical information about the incidence of ill-health in developing countries is still inadequate. Most accounts of disease patterns in these countries are impressionistic or rely on limited epidemiological surveys. Morbidity statistics are not collected systematically and only a few developing countries have adequate provisions for registering deaths; even where deaths are registered, the cause is frequently not known.

This is particularly true of infant deaths, which are grossly underreported.

Because of a paucity of data about morbidity and mortality, many epidemiologists rely on health-related demographic indicators when reporting on health conditions in the Third World. These indicators, which include crude death rates, infant mortality rates and estimates of life expectancy, do not provide information about the prevalence of disease but nevertheless allude to the health status of a population. Generally, high mortality, and especially infant mortality, coupled with low life expectancy, correlate with low health status and a high prevalance of communicable diseases.

Information about life expectancy and mortality in countries of different levels of development is summarised in Table 1.13. As may be seen in this table, there is a clear association between the level of development of a country and its performance on these indicators. The poorest countries have significantly higher crude death and infant mortality rates and significantly lower life expectancy. With the exception of the high-income oil exporting nations, performance on these indicators improves as the level of development increases.

Table 1.13: *Health-related demographic indicators, 1982*

Category	Life expectancy	Crude death rate	Infant mortality rate
Low-income developing countries	59	11	87
Middle-income developing countries	60	10	76
Upper-middle-income developing countries	65	8	58
High-income oil exporters	58	11	96
Industrial countries	75	9	10

Source: World Bank (1984).

Although the situation is still unsatisfactory, there have been noticeable improvements in health conditions as measured by the health-related demographic indicators in recent years. Before the Second World War, life expectancy in many developing countries was only about 32 years. By 1960, life expectancy had reached 44 years, and in 1970, 54 years; by 1980, it had risen to 55 years (World Bank, 1980). In the middle- and upper-middle-income developing countries, it had reached 60 years by this time. Similar improvements in crude death and infant mortality rates have been recorded in many developing countries. However, infant mortality in the developing countries as a whole is still many times higher than in the industrial nations and in the poorest countries, where the situation is depressing, infant mortality rates in excess of 100 per 1,000 are still recorded.

Two factors that have a profound impact on health are clean water and adequate sanitation. Most epidemiologists take the view that unsafe water supplies and poor sanitary facilities are a major cause of ill-health in the Third World. While most people in the industrial nations take clean water and sanitation for granted, both are still comparative luxuries in the Third World. The scarcity and inaccessibility of water involves many millions of women in the time-consuming and onerous task of fetching and carrying water to their homes. The burden of providing water for a family is revealed by the fact that an adult needs a minimum of 25 litres for daily use (Streeten *et al.*, 1981).

In investigating the water and sanitation problem in developing countries, the World Bank employed three criteria to determine adequacy of provision. Water must be 'safe' in the sense that it is uncontaminated by disease agents or harmful chemicals and it must be within 20 metres from the dwelling. Sanitary facilities must ensure the adequate disposal of wastes. In a survey of ninety-one developing countries in 1970, the World Health Organisation found that only 68 per cent of the urban population and 14 per cent of the rural population had adequate water supplies. Only 25 per cent of the urban population and 8 per cent of the rural population had adequate sanitary facilities. In some regions of the Third World, such as South Asia, these proportions were far lower (Saunders and Warford, 1976). Although the United Nations (1979) revealed that there had been a steady expansion of sanitary and water supply facilities during the 1970s, the situation is far from satisfactory. As Hardiman and Midgley (1982a) pointed out, there is a good deal of evidence to show that public waste disposal facilities in many developing countries do not operate effectively and that poor hygiene remains a major problem. In spite of the progress that has been made, Streeten *et al.* (1981) reported that water supply problems still affect many developing countries; they estimated that fewer than 500 million people in the Third World had adequate water and that the number without access is increasing.

Hunger and Food
It is very difficult to make accurate assessments of the extent of nutritional needs in the Third World. Reliable data about the incidence of malnutrition are not available and, in addition, it is difficult to define this concept. Because nutritionists disagree about the amounts of protein, calories and other substances required for a healthy diet, the criteria employed to define malnutrition in nutritional surveys vary, and it is difficult to compare findings. The relationship between hunger and food shortages is also complex. Although it would appear to be self-evident that food shortages are related to hunger, many developing countries with food surpluses nevertheless have a significant incidence of malnutrition.

It was shown earlier that rapid economic growth in many developing countries during the 1950s and 1960s was not always accompanied by simultaneous increases in agricultural production. Stagnating or falling agricultural output in many countries was also accompanied by a decline in food production. Table 1.14 provides information about food production trends since 1950. Compared with an index of 100 units for the 1960 to 1965 period, per capita food output rose by only seven points in the developing countries as a whole, and in the poorest countries, the increase was only four units. However, these data conceal the fact that in some countries, per capita food production actually declined. Worst affected were the African countries, where per capita food output fell by 10 per cent between 1965 and 1975 (Loup, 1983).

Table 1.14: *Food production indices, 1950–75*

Category	1950	1965	1975
Low-income developing countries	88	96	194
Middle-income developing countries	84	101	107
Industrial countries	84	102	115

Index = 100 units in 1960–65.
Source: Loup (1983).

The much-heralded Green Revolution was thought to offer a quick solution to the problem. Droughts in South Asia in the mid-1960s, and again in the early 1970s, spurred governments, and particularly the Indian government, to promote the new technologies. Although these policies had the desired effect, producing substantial grain surpluses, hunger has not been abolished. While India has been accumulating grain surpluses, average per capita food consumption has remained static for the simple reason that the country's poor could not afford to purchase more food. As these data reveal, food availability is not a guarantee that people will be well fed.

Various estimates of the incidence of malnutrition in the Third World have been published. The Food and Agricultural Organisation (1975) estimated that there were approximately 460 million malnourished people in the world in 1970. Power and Holenstein (1976) produced a lower estimate of 388 million for 1970, while Reutlinger and Selowsky (1976) suggested a figure of between 1,100 and 1,400 million in 1975.

There are differences of opinion also about whether or not the incidence of malnutrition has increased over the years. Because of a paucity of data for earlier periods, it is difficult to reach firm conclusions. Nevertheless, most authorities accept that there are more malnourished people in the world today than ever before. While some believe that this is largely due to population increases, others argue that the proportion of hungry people has increased as a result of stagnating incomes and declining food production in the poorest countries.

Estimates of the incidence of malnutrition are shown in

Table 1.15. Although these reveal that Asia has the highest incidence of malnutrition, it should be remembered that this datum is a function of the region's large population. As a proportion, the incidence of malnutrition is highest in Africa, affecting 25 per cent of the population. The estimated incidence of malnutrition in Central and South America was lower, but here a figure of 13 per cent is high given the region's relatively high per capita income.

Table 1.15: *Estimates of the incidence of malnutrition, 1970*

Region	Number (millions)	Percentage of population
Africa	68	25
Asia[a]	255	21
Central and South America	37	13
Industrial countries	28	3
World	388	14

a = excludes China.
Source: Power and Holenstein (1976).

Regional data conceal variations in the incidence of malnutrition in different countries. For example, Power and Holenstein (1976) reported that malnutrition is a serious problem in Haiti, even though people in the Caribbean as a whole are relatively well fed. Nor is the problem only confined to the poorest countries: El Salvador and Bolivia, which have relatively high per capita incomes, have a serious problem of malnutrition.

Within countries, hunger is concentrated among poor families and particularly among women and children; among women, the problem is most severe during pregnancy and periods of lactation. Malnutrition at this time is a major contributory factor in the high incidence of infant deaths in the Third World. The Brandt Report (Brandt *et al.*1981) noted that as many as 40 per cent of preschool children in the Third World are malnourished. Power and Holenstein (1976) suggested that between a half and two-thirds of children in the developing countries suffer from endemic hunger. Although data are limited, there is evidence to show that the elderly are also over-represented among the hungry.

The causes of hunger are complex, but most authorities now believe that poverty and inequality are highly significant factors in understanding its aetiology. The once-popular belief that malnutrition is caused by food shortages is no longer widely accepted. However, the relevance of this factor cannot be ignored. There is evidence to show that malnutrition increases as cash-cropping cultivation increases and as farmers neglect subsistence food production for monetary incomes. The spread of commercial, capital-intensive farming has increased the problem of landlessness, exacerbating the problem. Also, the spectre of famine is a real one. Nevertheless, while famines occur at discrete intervals, hunger is a daily experience for hundreds of millions of people in the modern world. The solution lies not in emergency responses to the crises of starvation but in determined social and political action and longer-term development programmes. In 1974 the World Food Conference resolved that 'within the decade, no child will go to bed hungry, that no family will fear for its next day's bread and that no human being's future and capacities will be stunted by malnutrition' (FAO, 1974). The decade has passed, but the ideals of the resolution are far from being realised.

Education and Literacy

Many social development experts regard the expansion of formal education in the developing countries as spectacular. Although Koranic and other forms of indigenous schooling were firmly established in the precolonial societies of the Third World, Western-style missionary education was limited to the few. The recognition that the possession of formal educational qualifications provided ready access to wage or salaried employment increased popular demand for the expansion of modern educational facilities and was also regarded by many independence leaders as a matter of national prestige. After decolonisation, many governments accelerated the trend towards educational expansion that had already begun before independence, producing a rapid

increase in the numbers of children on school enrolment
lists.

Working from United Nations and World Bank sources,
Hardiman and Midgley (1982a) estimated that there were
somewhat more than 70 million children and young people
in the educational systems of the developing countries in
1950. As shown in Table 1.16, this figure had almost trebled
to reach 200 million by 1965. Primary school enrolment
went up from 64 million to 160 million, while secondary and
tertiary enrolment also increased significantly. During this
period, government budgetary allocations to education
increased rapidly, reaching as much as 20 per cent of public
expenditure in many developing countries. After 1965,
however, the rate of expansion declined, particularly in the
primary sector. Although primary enrolment had increased
substantially by 1975, representing an increase of more than
300 per cent in twenty-five years, the annual rate of increase
halved from about 6 per cent in 1950 to 3 per cent in 1975.
On the other hand, tertiary enrolment, which increased
about ten times between 1950 and 1975, maintained its
increase of about 10 per cent per annum.

Table 1.16: *Expansion of the educational system in developing countries,*
1950–75

| Educational | Numbers (in millions) | | | % increase |
level	1950	1965	1975	since 1950
Primary	64.7	160.0	236.4	365
Secondary	7.5	36.6	69.0	920
Tertiary	0.9	3.5	9.5	1,056
All levels	73.1	200.0	314.9	431

Source: Hardiman and Midgley (1982a).

These increases have been accompanied by significant
improvements in literacy in the Third World. As shown in
Table 1.17, the proportion of adults who are literate has
increased from about 40 per cent in 1960 to nearly 60 per
cent in 1977. In 1950 the proportion was about a third. These
increases are widely regarded as remarkable. As Streeten *et*

al. (1981) observed, some 400 million people became literate in just fifteen years from 1960 to 1975.

Table 1.17: *Adult literacy, 1960–77*

Category	1960 (%)	1970 (%)	1977 (%)
Low-income developing countries	28	35	50
Middle-income developing countries	56	65	65
Third World	39	46	57
Industrial countries	98	99	99

Source: World Bank (1979, 1982).

While these overall trends are indeed impressive, they mask regional and national differences. Literacy rates vary significantly between the different world regions and are generally lowest in the poorest areas of the Third World. While literacy rates in Latin America increased from about 65 per cent in 1960 to 75 per cent in 1975, African rates increased from 20 to only 26 per cent during this period (Morawetz, 1977).

Another problem is that there are still many children who do not go to school. Streeten *et al.* (1981) calculated that for each child enrolled at school, there are three who do not attend. Many developing countries now publish primary school enrolment rates of 95 per cent or more, but these figures are misleading. Many children who are officially enrolled attend irregularly and many do not attend at all. Many are removed by their parents when they are old enough to work, and the drop-out rate is very high. Only a small proportion of primary school graduates will go on to the secondary level, and very few will reach university.

There is a good deal of evidence to show also that the quality of education in many developing countries is poor. Many teachers are inadequately trained, schools and colleges are often badly equipped and overcrowded, and staff morale is frequently low. There is concern also about the appropriateness of the curriculum. What Dore (1976) has called the 'diploma disease' is rife in many societies. Formal paper qualifications are widely regarded as being more important than skills and personal work fulfilment.

By stressing formal qualifications, the educational system becomes a mechanism for sifting people rather than a contributor to development. In many countries, particularly in South Asia, the emphasis on formal learning and on Western-style curricula has contributed directly to the growing problem of graduate unemployment.

Equally worrying are the inegalitarian effects of the educational system in many countries. Since educational policies often discriminate against women, the poorest groups and people who live in the rural areas, existing inequalities are amplified. Female primary school enrolment rates in many Third World countries are well below those for males, and in some societies they are very low indeed. The World Bank (1982) reported that female primary school enrolment rates were only 7 per cent in Afghanistan and Bhutan, 9 per cent in the Yemen Arab Republic and 15 per cent in Upper Volta. Enrolment rates for boys were significantly higher in each country. Unequal access to education not only perpetuates ignorance, but by restricting access to the poor, it exacerbates their disadvantage.

Shelter

Information about shelter conditions in the Third World is very inadequate. Few governments collect data about housing conditions, and international surveys are often dependent on dated and incomplete statistics. Also, housing experts disagree about the criteria which should be used to define adequate housing. The once widely-held view that shanty and other forms of self-constructed housing are by definition inferior and in need of demolition, has been challenged. Turner (1976), a leading authority on the subject, argued that so-called slum housing not only provides homes for millions of people in the Third World but is a viable solution to the housing crisis. If slum dwellers are given security of land tenure and assistance to improve their dwellings, they will contribute positively to the expansion of the housing stock.

Nevertheless, there is a good deal of evidence to show that housing conditions in the cities and rural areas of many developing countries are very poor indeed. Few shack dwellers have security of tenure, and many pay exhorbitant rents to landowners and even to other squatters who had previously staked their claim to the land. Urban dwellers in some cities, particularly in South Asia, have no homes at all and live permanently on the streets. Land concentration in many urban areas is marked, and politicians often have vested interests in land, effectively blocking the attempts of planners and housing authorities to provide more homes for the poor. Few governments have made any attempts to improve rural housing conditions, even though there is evidence to show that the problems of rural housing are as severe as those in the urban areas (United Nations, 1978).

One widely-used measure of housing conditions in the Third World is the proportion of the urban population living in slums and squatter settlements. Table 1.18 provides some statistical information on this aspect of the problem. Although the data given in this table are out of date and not very reliable, they do provide some insights into the extent of housing need. As shown in this table, many Third World cities have more than a third of their populations in slums and squatter areas. In many sub-Saharan cities, which are growing very rapidly indeed, the proportions are often more than 50 per cent.

Table 1.18: *Percentage of the urban population living in squatter settlements in selected Third World cities*

City	Country	%	Year
Amman	Jordan	12	1974
Baghdad	Iraq	25	1970
Bangkok	Thailand	15	1974
Blantyre	Malawi	56	1970
Bombay	India	45	1971
Brazilia	Brazil	41	1970
Buenos Aires	Argentina	5	1970
Calcutta	India	67	1971
Caracas	Venezuela	40	1974
Casablanca	Morocco	60	1971
Colombo	Sri Lanka	44	1972
Dacca	Bangladesh	18	1973
Dakar	Senegal	60	1971
Dar-es-Salaam	Tanzania	50	1970
Delhi	India	36	1971
Douala	Cameroon	87	1970
Guatemala City	Guatemala	30	1971
Ibadan	Nigeria	75	1971
Jakarta	Indonesia	26	1972
Karachi	Pakistan	23	1971
Kinshasha	Zaire	60	1970
Kuala Lumpur	Malaysia	37	1971
Lima	Peru	40	1970
Lome	Togo	75	1970
Manila	Philippines	35	1972
Mexico City	Mexico	46	1970
Nairobi	Kenya	33	1970
Ougadougou	Upper Volta	52	1972
Panama City	Panama	17	1970
Rio	Brazil	30	1970
Santiago	Chile	17	1973
Seoul	Korea	30	1970
Tegucigalpa	Honduras	25	1970

Source: Drakakis-Smith (1981), United Nations (1975).

2 The Origins of Welfare in the Third World

IDENTIFYING WELFARE

We have discussed earlier the scope of the term 'welfare' in the development context; if we are to consider welfare institutions we must take an equally broad approach to definition. It is not enough to deal only with those social institutions which are avowedly treating 'welfare' issues. This is of course so in all societies, and much recent work has been attempting to shift the attention of analysis to encompass all those institutions which contribute to the determination of patterns of welfare (George and Wilding, 1984). But in the societies of the Third World this is of even greater significance—operational distinctions between economic and social development activity are much less clear, and in very many instances demands for 'integrated social-economic development' set out to remove these distinctions altogether. As in all comparative work, great care must be taken not to transpose pre-existing categories to the analysis of institutions in other societies. Thus, this discussion will seek to identify themes and issues which are common in the emergence of formal welfare institutions in a range of societies the sheer scale of which really defies generalisation.

The difficulty of identifying those social institutions most relevant to welfare remains severe. Earlier discussion has demonstrated the range of needs which must be considered in Third World welfare—it is clear that we must be concerned, above all, with 'basic needs' as the heart of any

concept of welfare. Beyond that notion, which may of
course be interpreted in a variety of specific ways in different
societies, we must be concerned with a range of needs identified as 'welfare needs' and somehow distinguished from
other aspects of the totality of human needs. Clear examples
here are the need for the substitute care of children, and
the specific and unique needs of the physically disabled.
Both these groups of course have all the needs of the populations of which they are a part. But they do have specific
needs which conventionally have formed part of 'welfare';
essentially because welfare is irreducibly defined in terms of
responses to individual need. Thus, where there are services
and institutions which have as their purpose, or a major
part of their purpose, a response to the needs of these
groups, these must be considered. Particular examples will
be considered at greater length below. At this point an
immediate, and serious, difficulty may be identified: if the
scope of welfare is to be defined by reference to existing
institutions, then we are trapped within self-limiting and
stifling constraints.

We must consider institutions across a wide range of
'developmental' activity, on the one hand, but we must
clearly be concerned with conventionally defined welfare
institutions, which relate to very specific individual needs,
on the other. This crude characterisation of the spectrum
of institutions serves only to indicate the difficulty encountered in this area; there is in practice a tension between
these forces. First, there are those forces which seek to
direct attention and analysis to the very broadly defined
welfare institutions—frequently losing any distinctive
welfare concern and becoming the study of social aspects of
development in general. This is a perfectly legitimate, and
defensible position to adopt in the analysis of social welfare
in many Third World societies. Second, and fuelled by
demands of professionalism and the imperatives of operational classification and boundary-maintenance, there are
those forces which pull the concept of social welfare and its
study very firmly towards a narrow concentration on those
services, whether operated by the state or non-government
organisations, which are organised to respond to individual

needs—essentially 'social services'. This issue has been discussed quite widely (United Nations, 1968; 1970; 1979), but the tension continues, and its practical consequences are severe, not the least of them being a lack of coherent identity for 'welfare' in many countries, which seriously undermines the emergence of rigorous and sustained analysis.

Thus, as will emerge in later discussion, it is frequently the lack of a government agency with specific responsibility for welfare that limits the formulation of national plans or the implementation of programmes across a range of sectors. In very many instances the achievement of 'social development' is a frequently stated goal which remains at the level of rhetoric. We are concerned here to identify particular organised activities within the whole range of services and programmes administered by government and non-government agencies. An examination of the growth of those recognised as being charged with a responsibility for welfare will allow some elaboration of the present pattern of services and its consequences and limitations.

Before identifying some themes in the emergence of formal services it is necessary to indicate, in broad outline at least, the characteristics of provision for welfare prior to the relatively recent spread of organised welfare.

SOCIAL SUPPORT AND WELFARE IN TRADITIONAL SOCIETIES

The major force in the recent history of developing countries has been the impact of colonialism. For many countries this impact reaches back many centuries; for others, release from the direct impact of colonialism came some 100 to 200 years ago. For a few states (relatively very few) there has been no period of colonial rule. It remains the case that for the great majority of nation states, for at least the past 100 years there has been a substantial period of colonial rule. The experience of that rule varied enormously of course. There were substantial differences between colonial powers in the forms of administration and exploitation, the intensity of domination and the degree of social disruption (Wicker, 1958). Some of these differences will be explored further in later discussion of colonial welfare provision. What all communities under colonial rule had in common were pre-existing forms of social provision for the welfare of their members. This was rarely recognised by the incoming colonialists. Indeed, their perceptions of the societies upon which they imposed their administration were most often grossly distorted products of prejudice and ignorance.

Macnaught, in a history of British colonial rule in Fiji, quotes examples of such attitudes and beliefs among colonial officials, missionaries and others. For example, in the late 1890s there was agreement among the colonialists in Fiji that Fijian mothers were bad mothers—'a race of blunted sensibilities', claimed one official: ' "I have lived among natives during the past twenty-three years and have never seen any particular affection shown to a child by its mother" ' (Macnaught, 1976: 14). Such grotesque views were common; even the more enlightened among the colonialists believed themselves to be inherently superior to those into whose lands they had come. There was a profound lack of understanding of pre-existing traditions and social forms, except insofar as these were seen as 'obstacles to progress', and in particular to the progress of the Christian church and economic activity (Fanon, 1967; Rodney, 1972; Leys, 1975).

The ignorance of administrators and missionaries is of profound importance, for it was on the basis of that ignorance that so much was done in the name of welfare and education during the colonial period. Existing social arrangements were either seen as of no significance or as standing in the way of 'modern administration' (Ranger, 1969). These themes will be the subject of later discussion when contemporary issues in welfare—for example the role of traditional medicine in the provision of health services—will be seen to bear the legacy of those earlier perceptions and attitudes.

Another profound effect of this early denigration of pre-existing social systems (Cesaire, 1972) is that the conditions in pre-colonial society became extremely difficult to reconstruct. Later researchers faced enormous difficulties if they attempted to describe the patterns of social life in the period before the impact of the colonialists. There are many obvious reasons for this, extensively discussed elsewhere (Boahen, 1984). Several stand out as most important for our present discussion. First, the societies existing prior to the recent spread of European colonialism were, in most parts of the world, relatively small-scale communities without extensive written records of their own customs, traditions and history. The records they had, in oral and other forms, were inherently fragile and were often destroyed in the early stages of colonialism.

Second, later histories were most often based on the perverted accounts of 'explorers', early missionaries, traders and administrators concerned above all with the mainten-ance of law and order in what they perceived as hostile conditions. Such accounts were not only totally unrepresent-ative of the areas with which they purported to deal but were so influenced by the prejudices and attitudes referred to earlier as to be useless as anything other than as an indicator of the condition of the Europeans themselves. It was only in those societies with existing written traditions and other forms, which were able to survive the onslaught of colonialism, that the true nature of indigenous society could be conveyed to later generations relatively easily. In others, the barrier of 'colonial history' was a massive one, standing between people and their own cultural history (Fanon, 1967). A powerful contrast may be drawn here between the societies of sub-Saharan Africa and those of South-East Asia. Large parts of the regions were subject to colonial rule, but in the latter the existence of written traditions, and above all religious traditions, allowed a continuity of thought and expression despite the imposition of alien rule for long periods. In Africa, for example, it has taken many generations before Africans have been able to recapture their history and begin to rewrite the accounts of their past which were previously only available in the forms produced by the colonialists and those who relied primarily on the colonialists as their source (Mamdani, 1976; Morsy, 1984).

Related to this point is a third: the perceptions of present populations are the product of many forces; not the least of these forces, for the influential élites who control policies and programmes, is formal education. To the extent that such education has been of a kind which devalues, or perverts, traditions and social formations, and there is overwhelming evidence from around the world that it has been so, this will have a profound impact on the construction of history.

For some years, historians, anthropologists and others in developing countries have been attempting to bring together evidence which will allow a more genuine history of not only the formal administration of colonialism but the societies which preceded it (Worsley, 1984). Such work has a profound significance for our present discussion; it is in such work that we may find clues to the possibilities of human organisation in its myriad forms. For the fourth aspect of the difficulty of reconstructing precolonial social systems is the pervasive force of pressures which have consistently pushed societies in the direction of a defined 'modern' form, which was most profoundly rooted in the liberal Western ideal of 'individualistic, democratic man' in an essentially capitalist society. Thus there has been a long process of cultural imperialism which has been closely allied with economic imperialism—the reproduction of similar life-styles in widely differing parts of the globe is but the most superficial aspect of this continuing process. That recent years have witnessed reactions to this around the world, in attempts to recapture cultural values, traditions and forms is testimony to the power of underlying cultures. Nonetheless, it is difficult to overstate the general impact of this Western hegemony of life-style and perception. It continues to be produced and reinforced through education and literature, still overwhelmingly dominated by the institutions of relatively few industrialised countries.

Thus any attempt to identify the nature of traditional welfare is fraught with difficulty. It is only possible here to point to several of the most important themes.

The first is that the great majority of societies, prior to the period of colonial expansion, were ones in which individual needs were seen as part of the needs of the wider society. Social and economic organisation was complex and enduring, essentially able to combine flexibility of response to changes in the environment with persistent social structures and enduring values. Very many precolonial societies had precapitalist economies. They were not—neither are those societies which survive today—'primitive'. Such terminology is part only of foreign prejudice, and demonstrates nothing more than the ignorance of outsiders as to the real nature of societies they do not understand. Further, such views underline a fundamental point: traditional societies were based on quite different principles from those which inform the dominant value systems of the modern industrial states. Thus the first major theme is the dominance of communalism and collective effort in the organisation of precolonial societies. The household was the centre for production, distribution and consumption. Economies were largely organised around joint effort and cooperative work within extended families, clans, villages and similar communities. The overarching power of kinship ties in social relations provided an effective framework for the organisation and management of the household economy (Chowning, 1977; Constantine, 1977; Kayongo-Male and Onyanago, 1984).

Land and other productive resources were almost always owned and stored by the same traditional groupings. In most areas both subsistence production for consumption, and surplus wealth were produced communally. Complex patterns governed the disposition of wealth, but the most common pattern was one in which accumulated goods were held 'in trust' temporarily by leaders or other specified members of the society. The social forms governing the distribution and redistribution of these accumulations were absolutely fundamental to the maintenance of these societies and the interaction between them. Births, marriages, deaths, festivals, exchanges and trade were all means by which wealth was shared and patterns of obligation built and maintained. Such means of distribution frequently involved relatively distant communities and served to establish and reinforce bonds within and between communities (Davidson, 1967).

What is of vital importance to our present concern is that 'kinship' in traditional societies was a very broadly defined term involving both a much 'wider' concept than that familiar to the West, but also a concept much more profound in its force and the implications it carries for duties and obligations. Equally important, we must note that it was by the patterns of wealth distribution that economic equality and the material welfare of all were generally well maintained. Kinship relations were hardly distinguishable from property relations. Thus material welfare was essentially ensured to every member of the society at the level enjoyed by most other members of that society. Despite the enormous variation in form, this was the essential nature of traditional societies. The realities of life for the vast majority of people were bounded by the nature of local society and its forms and customs.

Equality in material conditions was also reflected in the vast majority of social and political systems. Whatever the extent of small-scale quarrels or even local wars over land and other resources, it was in most societies very unusual for anyone to be denied all access to the means of livelihood. Equally, the denial of material necessities or modest surpluses was extremely unusual. For the most part, and this is true of precolonial societies in all parts of the world, systems functioned well without accumulating permanent stocks of wealth under individual control.

This was not of course universally the case; examples abound of systems in which small numbers of the wealthy exploited, very often ruthlessly, large numbers of the poor. But again, the point must be made that for most people communities functioned at a relatively low level of material production, in ways which ensured more-or-less equal access to the means for life. It is in fact difficult to assess the level of material wealth in precolonial societies; there is of course a fundamental issue of definition here: what is 'wealth'? But in addition to such profound but intractable issues, there are more prosiac but nonetheless crucial ones. In very many parts of the world contemporary work has only recently literally 'uncovered' evidence of life-styles the quality of which has hitherto been unacknowledged and, in the absence of hard evidence, denied. Yet another example of the imposition of alien perceptions on the reality of other societies. The recapturing of the past extends far back in time, and ethno-archaeology is now beginning, in the hands of the people themselves, to aid that recapture. What evidence there is then supports the view that pre-existing societies were considerably richer than previously assumed—richer that is in the quality of lives led, the levels of sophistication in art, music and cultural forms, the complexity of social formations and relationships with the environment.

These societies worked without large-scale inheritance, wage labour or any dominant profit motive. There was no mass production, no business empires and no personal fortunes. Neither were there extremes of exploitation or great and lasting contrasts between rich and poor families. But neither was there economic growth.

The communalism of traditional societies, the 'cooperation' and mutual support of each member by each other member through the certain function of established forms governed by known and powerful social values is a profound theme in any discussion of welfare in traditional societies. But this is not an uncontentious area: there has been considerable dispute about the 'reality' of this view. The purpose here is not to romanticise the past but to establish as clearly as possible that in economies in which affective ties prevail—what Hyden refers to as an 'economy of affection'—there is an element of reciprocity that is structurally induced and maintained (Hyden, 1980: 19). That reciprocity is what concerns us here, but there is debate as to its extent and its nature.

This debate is echoed around the world; the nature of precolonial society is the subject of intense argument. This is so not least because of contemporary attempts to invoke the past as the justification for present and future policies and programmes. But the search for some indisputable truth about the nature of past societies is surely a chimera; the nature of those societies is beyond reach in anything but broad outline. What we have, then, from historical evidence and those societies which have survived until relatively recently with little or no outside influence, is a picture dominated by communal activity and intense relationships between individuals and the groups in which they lived. All members of communities had roles, and these roles were known, defined and ordained by the group. The needs of the individual, in terms of 'welfare' were therefore satisfied as a normal function of the group as a whole.

As late as the 1920s, the force of this communalism was still evident in Fiji. As part of the colonial administration's effort to destroy Fijian culture and society to allow more rapid expansion of the colonial economy there was an attack on these values of cooperation and communal responsibility. The differences between those values and the ones the colonialists wished to implant are shown clearly in the following statements made by the Colonial Secretary and Receiver General:

The basis of the inertness of the Fijian is to my mind, due to . . . an overburden of communalism, and the difficulty of individual Fijians to assert and maintain individualism. . . . the perpetuation of the communal system . . . is a retrogression . . . [the Fijian] should develop sufficiently to be able to live and support himself and his dependents as units of the community European civilisation has evolved [Macnaught, 1976: 134].

Thus the entry of colonial administration, and especially the colonial economy, came into direct conflict with a pattern of social relations which put primary emphasis on group responsibility for welfare, patterns of obligation and reciprocity and acknowledgement of social value regardless of material criteria. There was, therefore, from the early colonial period a constant tension between sets of values which were rooted in quite different perceptions of the relationship between individuals and the communities of which they are a part. Some aspects of this tension will be discussed later when contemporary issues in social policy are examined and will be seen to carry the burden of contradictions between these radically different sets of values.

The following set of contrasts, produced as part of a

training programme for community workers in Papua New Guinea, is a specific illustration of this general issue.

Contrasting Perceptions of Basic Values

Some Typical Traditional Melanesian Characteristics Or Goals	Some Typical Western Social Characteristics or Goals
The traditional Melanesian societies sought to preserve a state of stability, balance, harmony. Above all, the leaders struggled to keep their group intact as a society, to survive as a people. This usually meant guarding against change. The strong communal bonds were emphasised. Individualism was considered threatening, and was frowned upon.	Most modern western societies prefer an open society with capacity to change. Individualism is encouraged. There is great mobility, with persons free to find 'community' on their own terms. Privacy is valued. Bonds of kinship are often very weak. Security is often based on a job or on the nuclear family.
Children were educated informally and practically right in the village to take clearly defined roles which reinforced the bonds of kinship and interdependence.	Children are educated formally in classrooms, often rather theoretically, often away from the immediate community, with a great diversity of roles, opportunities for specialization.
Leaders, or 'big men' emerged through a complex informal process, usually an unspoken process, to defend the group, organise the people, settle disputes, and manifest personally the wealth, dignity, and strength of the group	Politics are highly developed, formal. Leaders are elected through a clearly defined process, with leadership centred more on intellectual rather than physical qualities. The leaders don't carry the great range of functions, as in Melanesian societies. A great deal of 'delegating' takes place.
Relationships with outside persons and groups were entered into very cautiously over a long period of time.	Relationships with other persons and groups tend to be entered into easily, but are less personal, more superficial, more easily broken.
Objective concepts of right or wrong did not really thrive. Behaviour was promoted which supported kinship obligations and customs more than any particular moral code. Enforcement was carried out through social pressures. Conflict within the group was	Most western societies tend to be rather moralistic (at least most of them have rather highly developed laws and moral codes even if they're not closely followed in practice!). Enforcement is quite formal, with more emphasis on punishment than on reconciliation.

minimized, but conflict with outsiders was quite common. Identifying with a side of 'right' was not nearly so important as identifying with wantoks. Handling of conflict within the group was more concerned with reconciliation than with punishment.

The ground was not only a place on which to live and produce. It was the seat of cultural ties, the focal point for human relationships, cultural values, language, ambitions. A specific geographical place where a person has his physical and spiritual roots, was the place of one's ancestors, the location of the familiar myths handed down from one generation to the next. It could not be owned by any one individual, and 'sale' or lease of land meant something far different and less absolute than in the western sense of the word.

Land is primarily a place on which to live, a place from which you can do business, or a resource for production. It is seen for its usefulness, not for its sentimental value or religious significance. Individuals can often own land and do almost anything they want with it--divide it, sell it to anyone, destroy its usefulness if they please. It's interesting that in very densely populated countries such as The Netherlands, Israel, Japan, however, we see land laws coming back to tribal-type controls.

The primary economic goals were subsistence and prestige. Through communal enterprise food was grown and collected. There was much sharing, little storing. Capital was accumulated in the form of food (usually pigs) or money (such as shell money) which could buy food, and in a highly ritualistic fashion was directed in most complicated ways to achieve situations which might return maximum prestige. Prestige was often visibly measured in terms of pigs and women.

Economic goals of most western societies, as in Melanesian societies, might be seen in terms of subsistence and prestige. However, they are usually more simple and direct: earning money to improve physical comfort, convenience, security, prestige. Wealth is defined differently. The house, the clothing, the car, the electrical appliances are all visible signs or criteria of success or failure. Pursuit of success is carried out in highly individualistic manner. Sharing is limited usually to the nuclear family, there is much saving, much accumulation of wealth by individuals. Capital is often accumulated for the purpose of enhancing earning capacity.

Exchange was not mainly for the purpose of obtaining consumer

Exchange is very practical, not ceremonial, usually based on cash, goods—it served to maintain balance, to bring about sharing, to play out 'one-upmanship'.

and is seldom subject to group control.

The economy as a system was not dynamic, but was rather static or changeless.

The economic system is highly dynamic, very subject to change and fluctuation.

Division of labour was mainly between men and women. There was otherwise very little specialization or division.

A high degree of specialization is found.

Religious and secular goals were highly integrated. Religious knowledge gave power for economic and other forms of success. Religion was a community matter, not just an individual matter. Sharing, rather than obedience to a religious code, was stressed. Fulfilment was seen in terms of this worldly life, not in another unseen life.

In most western societies there is a clear separation of the sacred and the secular. Religion is a private, individual matter, often, with even the family avoiding interference with individual religious preferences. Religion often aims at fulfilment in some other life, rather than this one.

[Papua New Guinea, National Youth Movement, 1981, n.p.)

SOCIAL CHANGE AND SOCIAL POLICY

As we have seen, the question of state provision for welfare arose for the first time as an issue during the colonial period. Before then, the household community, the extended family and other larger groups acted as institutions for the provision of individual care, material support or the satisfaction of other needs. Colonial rule, wherever it was imposed, set in motion forces of change which transformed not only traditional economies but also their associated social institutions and social relations. The traditional organisations which had ensured economic provision not just for individuals but for the whole community became radically altered. Above all, as the patterns of change engendered and forced through by colonialism began to take a more complete hold, even on local communities; individual support was progressively detached from the concerns of the household, the extended family and the kinship-based community. The dislocations of economic and social change, the rise of new demands for labour and new dispositions of material resources were all part of a decline in the capacity of extended families and local communities to support their own members to the extent to which this had been possible in the past. But of more profound significance to the issues with which we are concerned, there was the insidious growth of individualism and privatisation of responsibility suggested earlier. MacPherson (1982) discussed the nature of colonial administration in relation to welfare services which were seen to be related primarily to two imperatives. First, the perceived need to ensure that suitable conditions for economic activity were established and maintained. Second, and inextricably linked with the first, was the notion of 'the civilising mission'. It was this which not only provided the basis for much of the welfare work which was undertaken but also provided the justification for the consistent destruction of pre-existing cultures and social formations as 'uncivilised'. As Joseph Chamberlain said of the 'duty' of the British as colonialists, 'We develop new territories as trustees for civilisation, for the commerce of the world' (quoted by Mair, 1984: 2).

These two forces behind colonialism were of course in direct contradiction, the one with the other. In the drive to allow entry to the 'commerce of the world', wide-ranging and profound social dislocation was not simply inevitable but vitally necessary if productive forces were to be released from their traditional constraints and formations. But the nature of the administrations, reflecting as they did an exaggerated version of what was thought to characterise the values of the industrial states of the nineteenth century, had no intention of taking responsibility for the consequences of social disruption. There can be no doubt that the social disruption was profound. Davidson describes the pattern in Africa:

Gradually, as the colonial years rolled by, Africa's deepening dependence on the outside world was accompanied by other developments. Old confusions expanded into new confusions. Labour migration, land expropriation, and all the dislocations that went with them, gradually wrecked the earlier stabilities of African community life and reproduced although of course in new and different forms, the ancient miseries of the slave trade [Davidson, 1984: 212].

Of course, it must again be emphasied that the states with which we are now concerned have each had their own unique history; not all have had direct colonial rule, many had major urban centres for centuries, a number had complex and enduring national systems of government and administration long before the influence of the West. While all this is true and is of crucial importance in understanding the past development and present form of social issues and the response to them in terms of organised welfare it still remains the case that we can observe a number of basic trends in the nature of social change (Long, 1977).

The African example is extreme; the present tragedies on that continent may be the result of many factors, but there can be no denial that a major force behind contemporary disasters is the legacy of past disruption. What was the genesis of that disruption and its successors? Davidson argues that by the 1950s the instability and social change which resulted from the expansion of the colonial economies and their relationship with the metropolitan countries had 'gathered into a profound crisis affecting every part of African society' (Davidson, 1984: 212). Many rural areas were short of food and labour, the towns were unable to cope with those driven from the countryside. Above all, he claims, there was confusion, disarray and uncertainty. None of this was propitious for independence, which the great majority of African states gained in the late 1950s and early 1960s; none of this, suggests Davidson, was intended by anyone, least of all the colonial officials.

The economies of the colonies had never been strong, being almost always tied to very few primary products. Those economies were furthermore internally weak, being oriented almost exclusively to metropolitan markets and little concerned with the growth of indigenous production for consumption or development. Thus the economic disasters of the 1920s and 1930s had shattered the colonial economies. What little prosperity had found its way to the people was snatched back, and organised social welfare services, to the small extent that these had been established by the 1930s, were severely cut back (Boahen, 1984). Reports from all the colonies repeated the refrain that economic circumstances often did not allow the maintenance of services, and certainly did not allow the expansion of services or the establishment of new ones. The slump of the 1930s had profound effects on the colonies of Africa; the impact was only muted for the majority of people because the level of services and development assistance had already been so low (Constantine, 1984).

As the 1930s brought some improvements in the economies of the West and some signs of the end of the slump, there were changes in colonial policy. In Britain, by far the major colonial power in Africa, there was a major shift in official attitudes. There were many reasons for this shift, but as so often, the immediate catalyst for change was a threat to public order. There was serious rioting in the West Indies in the late 1930s which brought the appointment of a Royal Commission to investigate the condition of the British colonies in that part of the world. Its report described them as 'a tropical slum', and led the Colonial Office to press, successfully, for the abandonment of the principle that all the colonies must be self-supporting and the allocation of resources by the Treasury for 'development and welfare' (Constantine, 1984). It was in the Colonial Development and Welfare Act of 1940 that this was translated into the beginnings of formal organised welfare in the British colonies.

But this shift came just as the West was preparing for war; the long period of terrible destruction and suffering had many consequences for Africa, as it did for the great majority of the colonies around the world. In terms of the radical social changes with which we are concerned, the most important single consequence was the mobilisation of the colonies as part of 'the war effort'. To some extent this involved the recruitment of men for the armies of the West; although relatively small-scale, the impact of this was profound. Of much more immediate impact was an intensification of production demanded of rural producers. As part of that drive for production, many of the constraints which had held the most extreme actions in check during peacetime, were taken off. Davidson quotes a Jesuit priest speaking in 1945 on what had been happening in the Belgian Congo:

For five years, our populations were subjected to an extremely intense and varied war effort. The whole black population was mobilised to produce as much as possible as fast as possible, in order to send the Allies what they needed and make good the loss of imports . . . only coercion enabled us to reach the end of the war without great damage [Van Wing, quoted by Davidson, 1984: 213].

It was not until the period of reconstruction after the war that efforts at 'development' really began. But these were extremely limited and paid only a minimal attention to social development or the social welfare services. The fundamental social changes wrought by long periods of colonial rule, forced economic change, alienation of land and the other dimensions of the European presence were not the subject of coherent analysis or planned response. Such responses as there were sought to contain real and imagined threats to public order and the threats to property posed by the growing numbers of the dispossessed, especially in the towns (MacPherson, 1982). The beginnings of organised welfare services primarily concerned with law and order and social control will be examined later when the contemporary pattern of welfare services is discussed.

The African example serves to illustrate in broad outline the major trends in social change—economic and social dislocation, urbanisation, and the erosion of pre-existing communities with the attendant destruction of pre-existing capacities for social welfare. More specifically, what were the changes in social life which most directly affected the welfare of individuals, families and communities? These have been indicated earlier, in discussion of contrasting values, but might usefully be discussed in a little more detail here. Again, generalisation is difficult and dangerous. No two parts of the world have experienced the same pattern of change; we can only look for common themes which will be expressed in very different ways in different contexts.

The case study which follows illustrates many of the issues

already identified; it does not however deal with the whole range of welfare needs and responses but concentrates on social services for the most part. Nonetheless, it serves to bring together elements of social change as experienced by individuals and families, together with some discussion of social policy responses in a particular setting. Broad trends in the development of formal welfare institutions will be outlined at the end of this chapter; some more detail of the historical development and contemporary nature of specific services will be found in Chapter 5.

SOCIAL CHANGE AND SOCIAL WELFARE: A CASE STUDY

An illuminating example of such change is provided by a small Pacific society—the Gilbert and Ellice Islands. In an account, written in 1972, Morris Fox discussed at length the nature and extent of 'social welfare problems and needs' (Fox, 1976: 54–73). The territory was then a British colony and was later divided into the Gilbert Islands and Tuvalu. The reports of social conditions, and responses to them, are interesting not least because they were written in the early 1970s, when the examples of many other countries were available for comparison. They were also compiled, of course, with the perception, and preconceptions, of that period. But, most important for our present purpose, the patterns of social change observed, and their consequences, must be seen as typical in essence of such changes in communities around the world, albeit with some variations in the specific forms, and the scale of the social systems under consideration. But, yet again, it is important to emphasise that for the vast majority of the world's population, small-scale communities and relatively local geographical and social contexts are the major determinants of the nature and quality of life. Failure to appreciate this has bedevilled a great many attempts to comprehend social conditions and has certainly undermined organised programmes intended to improve those conditions (Chambers, 1984; Mair, 1984). The other feature of this case study is that the changes described took place very much later in the South Pacific than in other parts of the world. In the account here, it may be possible to see the sort of change which has occurred in communities in very many parts of the world over a very long period, but most intensively over the past 100 years.

In 1972, Fox reported that:

> There appears to be an awareness among many segments of the population of both the scope and nature of social breakdown occurring throughout much of the Colony, though these may be expressed in different terms. The level of concern seems high among community leaders, both in and out of government. However there is an impression that many people neither recognise the seriousness of what is happening nor the adjustments that will have to be made to successfully cope with the breakdown occurring. As one would expect, informants were having difficulty separating problems from symptoms and were inclined to over-simplify both possible causes and likely solutions [Fox, 1976: 54].

A number of special issues were identified as being of particular significance in the social conditions found in the Colony at the time of the report.

Social Change
Nearly all Fox's informants gave examples of the ways in which the traditional life-style and its attendant value systems had changed and were continuing to change. Those changes were seen to be accompanied by conflict, anxiety, growing distance between generations, identity problems and, in some instances, anti-social behaviour. Related to these changes it was argued was the increasing challenge to traditional authority and established discipline patterns. A number of factors were seen to be important here: the growing availability of independent sources of income being important insofar as it allowed individuals to separate themselves from the extended family and wider social groups. The previously existing sanctions which controlled behaviour could not be applied as powerfully as before. But outside influence was also identified as important in undermining traditional authority; alien mass media were being imported, and in particular foreign educational programmes were seen to be influential. Islanders themselves were

becoming 'agents of change' as they gained Europeanised educations, became paid workers and, in a number of cases, travelled abroad to return with impressive tales and imported goods. In Fox's words, 'The commercial mass media are seen as an effective form of cultural subversion'.

So a general pattern of rapid cultural change was established. The pace of change was in itself a problem, but very many people, particularly the older generations saw in the *content* of that change cause for concern. Whatever the long-term consequences of the displacement of traditional cultural values by those associated primarily with a Western consumerist culture, the short-term consequences of this were felt very keenly. Whatever the scale of these effects, that these were the perceptions held by the people themselves was important, as were the trends identified. The implications for existing and future welfare needs and responses were clear:

As a consequence of all this, one hears that children and youth are defying their elders, families are resisting taking discharged chronically ill patients back into their homes, family income is diverted to such non-essentials as alcoholic beverages and imported starchy foods; some gardens are untended, theft and vandalism are on the increase and there is general discontent with the level of living that can be financed by the Gilbertese and Ellice Islanders themselves with no aid from other countries [Fox, 1976: 54].

Population Imbalance and Migration
The movement of people and the consequent redistribution of the population was seen by local people as a major factor contributing to social breakdown. Specifically, migration was associated with urban congestion, seen as undesirable and unhealthy in comparison with traditional patterns of settlement. This embryonic urbanisation was further regarded as the source of a lowering of moral standards, weakening of the mutual assistance pattern, depletion of the more productive manpower in the rural areas, imbalance of sex ratios (especially among the 18 to 35 age group), decline in food production, marital discord, unmarried parenthood, child neglect, and increased juvenile delinquency and adult crime. A number of people felt that the

colonial administration had itself contributed substantially to this population imbalance by its practice of centralising its facilities and services in one major administrative centre. Internal migration was widely seen as the most pressing problem facing the colony, as it has been, and continues to be, in very many discussions of social conditions in the poor countries of the world.

The reasons given for migration to the town mirror those described elsewhere (Abhu-Lughod and Hay, 1979; Levine and Levine, 1979; Lloyd, 1979). In the Gilbert and Ellice Islands people were moving to South Tarawa for many reasons: for wage-employment, to attend a better school, get training, get medical care and visit friends and relatives. These were major reasons; there were in addition a number of other suggestions as to why people moved. Again these are suggestive both of the infinite complexity of migration but also of the underlying nature of social life and conditions, both in the rural areas and the towns. There is a clear theme here in the desire, particularly among the young, and women, to break free, at least for a period, of precisely that web of traditional obligation, duty and responsibility which we have seen as serving to maintain the welfare of the community:

factors inducing migration include . . . wealthier relatives, more cinemas, more night life, readily accessible liquor, less surveillance by traditionalists, more fun, escape from the drudgery of maintaining gardens, 'find' a husband, avoiding marital conflict, better chances for sports, bigger crowds to mix in, freedom from church obligations, leaving school failures behind, avoidance of being 'kept down' by adults, escape from boredom, more freedom for women [Fox, 1976: 57].

With regard to the social problems created by the overcrowding associated with this migration, the local people described conditions familiar in very many parts of the world. It is striking here, as elsewhere, that many of the features of an overcrowded urban environment cited as cause for concern are at the same time among those things which attract migrants to the town. It is of course this essential dilemma that lies at the heart of the social changes we are concerned with. Many features of urbanisation, and other major social changes, are both desirable and destructive at the same time:

houses crowded too close together, too many occupants per dwelling, shortage of land for family subsistence, inadequate play areas, increased pollution, lack of privacy, over-exposure of children to cinemas, dance halls and bars, gangs of unemployed and idle youth and men, neglected and delinquent children, shortage of places in schools, heavy burden of relatives being supported by wage earners, need to buy more imports, and rising costs of government services [Fox, 1976: 57].

Problems were not confined to the town, however; out-migration from the rural areas was seen to be the cause of major social disruption there also, and may again be seen as having particular relevance for social welfare concerns and the formulation of social policies. Due to the out-migration of males, there was a shortage of labour for food production and other work. There was sex imbalance, family break-up, an increase in infidelity and unmarried parenthood. In a more general sense, and clearly related to the issues of cultural change discussed earlier, there was a 'loss of cultural vitality, feeling of being "left behind", and sense of geographical and social isolation' [Fox, 1976: 57].

Deteriorating Level of Living
Any discussion of 'levels of living' is fraught with difficulty, and much work has been devoted to attempting to establish measures of such levels and changes in them (Hilhorst and Klatter, 1985). In the Gilbert and Ellice Islands, many people were concerned in the early 1970s that the spreading social breakdown was associated with a poorer quality of life. It is interesting to note that this trend was measured not by any physical standard, which for those in the cash economy had improved, but by reference to other factors. Among the features of contemporary life which were identified in this way were having to live in an unplanned community, seeing the environment polluted, suffering loss of pride because of being dependent on others rather than being self-sufficient, experiencing family separation and the generation gap, observing disoriented and deviant children and youth, watching the dying heritage of the past, seeing

misuse of leisure time, having sources of traditional foods neglected and feeling the mounting pressure of excess population. Such dimensions of social life and consciousness are extremely difficult to measure but may very often be of much more importance in defining the quality of life, as experienced by individuals, than are some of the factors more amenable to measurement and thus more attractive to policy-makers and planners.

Unemployment and Underemployment
There was a growing army of unemployed, primarily men and boys—migrants without work, school-leavers and students waiting for places in school. There was insufficient land in or near the town to support subsistence farming by the unemployed; to some extent unemployment was the result of lack of education or training, but the vast majority were reported to be idle because there were not enough job. There was no accurate count of the unemployed.

Family Breakdown
There was a conviction that the number of separated families had grown considerably, especially due to migration. Another perceived indication of family breakdown was the increasing evidence of neglected elderly persons. This was seen as a recent development, and one that was at odds with traditional patterns of family life. It was felt that the scale of this problem was greatly underestimated because the elderly did subsist, kept very much to themselves and were often not visible to the public. This was seen to be a consequence of scattered families with little communication, together with reluctance on the part of the older persons to become a burden on others outside their own families.

Similarly, a growing gulf was reported between very many children and their parents. European culture, with an emphasis on permissiveness and the emancipation of youth, was seen to be in conflict with traditional authoritarian styles of family life. There was considerable pressure on children to succeed in the formal education system and what was seen as a growing tendency to neglect those who did not.

Such neglect was largely in terms of a lack of close supervision and was of significance only in the urban areas. In relation to juvenile delinquency, it was widely felt that there were two major factors affecting the perceived rise in offences committed by young people. First there was a belief that lack of adequate supervision was fundamental; some parents no longer took responsibility for the actions of their children. Second, the influence of imported Western mass media was felt to be significant: 'the repeated exposure of children to movies which depict bizarre and shocking behaviour probably has a cumulative effect of undermining the value systems established by the children's own culture and thus contributes to their deviant behaviour' (Fox, 1976: 56).

In this outline of aspects of change as perceived in the Gilbert and Ellice Islands we have seen a number of themes which recur in accounts of social welfare. Health and education were not referred to directly but will be discussed later. It is not suggested that the pattern indicated here is universal, but it does find echoes in very many accounts from around the world (Thursz and Vigilante, 1975, 1976; Hardiman and Midgley, 1982a). Finally, it is useful to indicate the response, in terms of social welfare policies and programmes, to the problems identified. There was recognition of 'the necessity for balancing economic with social planning and balancing planning for education and health services with planning for social welfare services' (Fox, 1976: 61). It was hoped that a strengthening of human services would help to prevent, reduce and alleviate the various forms of social breakdown and encourage and support a better quality of community life. The arguments used to justify an expansion of social welfare services were essentially those of the period—a human resources case together with notions of prevention. As discussed elsewhere, there was a significant shift away from remedial social welfare, at least at the level of rhetoric. It was still the case, however, that in 1972 there was particular emphasis on the threat, present and future, from delinquency and crime.

Present patterns of social welfare services have a considerable part of their roots in economic necessity and the desire to maintain social order. We have seen that the origins of welfare lie not just in organised services but in the patterns of social relationships and obligations which existed prior to the relatively recent predominance of Western economic power and associated influences. The disruption of pre-existing communities and the contradictions between traditional and introduced value systems are common themes in the origins of organised welfare systems. For above all, it is as a collective response to social need that welfare must be seen.

FORMAL WELFARE INSTITUTIONS

As noted earlier, welfare institutions were formed to an extremely limited extent during the colonial period. The non-government organisations, especially the missions, formed a large proportion of such institutions, but their impact, although relatively great, was in absolute terms very slight. Across the range of welfare concerns the formal institutions had a number of key features in common. Above all, the imperatives of economic expansion, together with the maintenance of social order determined the nature and extent of social provisions. The primacy of economic development, oriented to metropolitan interests determined both the location and the nature of welfare institutions. Health, education, housing and social welfare facilities and services were provided for employees in the formal wage economy in order to maximise productivity and minimise disruption. Both state and mission facilities tended to follow the geographical pattern of economic activity and expansion, if for no other reasons than obvious ones of ease of transport, concentration of population and maintenance of control. Thus facilities were found in settlements and towns, in plantations and mines, and along major roads or the 'line of rail'. But the primacy of economic development also determined the nature and extent of welfare institutions, as we have seen. Such programmes were seen as peripheral and residual; provision was to be made at the minimum level possible consonant with a response to the problem perceived. Thus only the most pressing problems were to be the concern of organised welfare. This was as true in health as it was in social services or education. Compounded with an insistence on self-financing in the colonies and a predominant view that the state should have a restricted role in welfare, this resulted in an extremely low level of services, dominated by a minimalist, residual approach.

The nature of colonial administrations gave emerging welfare institutions distinctive features which heavily influenced policy-making. Administrations were highly bureaucratised and extremely centralised, heavily dependent on an authoritarian legal system and staffed almost entirely by foreigners from the metropolitan countries. Such administrations were essentially designed for control; the maintenance of order and the downward transmission of policies formulated elsewhere were their primary tasks. Clearly there were many instances of imaginative and progressive activity within colonial administrations, especially at the local level first, as there were very many instances of horrific exploitation, barbarous treatment and gross incompetence. But the nature and dynamics of national welfare institutions were set by the character of colonial administrations and their approach to welfare (MacPherson, 1982).

In more specific terms, those welfare institutions which were established were clearly permeated by imported Western approaches, values, attitudes and beliefs. In the period after the Second World War especially, there was considerable growth in health and education, and to some extent in social services (Mair, 1944; Kulkarni, 1979). Services were staffed with specialists from the metropolitan countries who had enormous influence on the emerging welfare institutions.

Thus, before independence most countries had only very sketchy welfare institutions. Health and education were characteristically more fully developed than any others. Housing was almost universally linked with wage employment, social services were minimal and concerned primarily with responses to urban crime (Hardiman and Midgley, 1982a; MacPherson, 1982). The resources made available to welfare were pitifully small, with the state reducing its responsibility still further by encouraging non-government organisations, in all fields (United Nations, 1965).

With independence these features continued to dominate; patterns of social policy and social welfare administration were still shaped by the past but also by the continuing force of outside influence. A brief examination of the constraints on policy-making in the newly independent states is necessary to an understanding of how contemporary welfare institutions continue to be shaped by forces inimical to genuine development.

As we have seen, although there was great variation in the level of resources available to colonial economies, they shared a common feature in that the monetised sector was organised primarily for export production. Infrastructure and state activity were oriented accordingly. Newly independent states had very few real possibilities for reorientation away from export production and from external dependence—certainly not in the short run and certainly not if they sought rapid increases in foreign earnings with which to begin new programmes including social welfare. Existing programmes, with their firmly established administrations and staffing were not easily open to reorientation or even to restriction. Colonial societies were marked by gross inequality; at independence economic stratification remained along with patterns of social segregation and élite privilege. Access to formal education, housing, hospital-based health services and other social resources was grossly distorted in favour of small élite groups.

The state itself was a colonial concept, imposed upon precolonial societies with little regard for their own structures and boundaries except where precolonial states were useful to indirect rule. The scope of state activity was wide, but it directly affected a small minority. In all colonies, the state embodied a form of infrastructure and administrative system closely integrated with the mobilised sectors of society. This feature was pre-eminent in the post-independence period when power had moved to indigenous hands.

Until the last years of colonialism, policy-making positions were restricted to those recruited from the metropolitan countries. When local people were allowed into these roles it was only those who had been socialised into the values and orientation of the colonial public service through long experience in subordinate positions or qualified through higher education. Localisation of the public service did not imply institutional change, and indeed in the great majority of states there was very little such change.

Since the nation state was essentially a colonial artefact, its patterns of resource allocation, welfare institutions and social policies were largely determined by colonial assumptions and priorities. A fundamentally limiting factor in the immediate post independence period was the general assumption that the colonial state must be maintained; it might be redirected or reoriented but not radically reshaped. Thus the pattern of formal welfare institutions established during colonialism survived through independence, and in most states was strengthened in an expression of the desire to extend services. The pervasive values and approaches which had flowed in from outside continued to influence policies, the process becoming more powerful but less visible as localisation brought the replacement of foreign policy-makers with local policy-makers (Midgley, 1981). As we shall see, these influences continue and are a major theme in the contemporary analysis of social policy. Ballard, in an examination of policy-making in new states, identified both the limitations on change and a key factor in successful examples of such change:

Developing or reorienting services . . . meant developing new capacity to spend funds. It required substantial commitment to changing the impact of services—and therefore of state impact on society—to alter inherited patterns, and this normally depended on mobilized political will outside the confines of the public service [Ballard, 1981: 9].

Part II
Analytical Significance of Third World Social Policy

3 The Study of Third World Social Policy

The previous section of this book was intended to provide an empirical introduction to the issues that concern Third World social policy investigators. Its discussion of the nature and extent of social need and historico-descriptive review of the emergence and present features of welfare institutions in the developing countries was intended not only to summarise the subject matter of Third World social policy but to foster a greater appreciation of the complexities of the phenomena that scholars working in the field are seeking to explain.

In this second part of the book, an attempt will be made to show how Third World social policy investigators have dealt with their subject matter. It will, in particular, seek to review their attempts to invoke analytical models and theories which account for welfare phenomena in generalised, conceptual terms. As noted in the Introduction to this volume, social policy's theoretical development is still hampered by a parochial preoccupation with trends in the industrial countries. Few propositions which transcend the experiences of these countries and which have universal relevance have gained currency within the subject. Although some Third World social policy investigators have borrowed established theoretical models from the corpus of Western social policy research to account for events in the developing countries, few of these models have been vigorously tested in the broader empirical field of the Third World. It is a major objective of this part of the book to consider the relevance of these theories to the Third World and to examine the significance of Third World social policy research for theoretical speculation in the subject as a whole. In this way, it is hoped, this book may contribute to the emergence of a wider global perspective in social policy studies.

But first, it may be useful to summarise briefly the nature of Third World social policy research as an academic enterprise. By reviewing the writings of different scholars engaged in the field, insights may be obtained into the topics they have covered and the various approaches they have used. This exercise will also provide the necessary background for the discussion in Chapter 4.

THE LITERATURE OF THIRD WORLD SOCIAL POLICY

Western social policy investigators often assume that very little research has been undertaken into the welfare institutions of the developing countries. It is widely believed that this is a major reason for the virtual absence of references to these countries in the leading American and British textbooks on comparative social welfare. With the publication and circulation in recent years of books on Third World social policy by British authors such as Hardiman and Midgley (1982a), MacPherson (1982) and Midgley (1981, 1984a), more social policy investigators in the industrial countries have become aware of the existence of a literature on the subject. But while many believe that these works have ventured into a new and previously unexplored field to create a new specialism in social policy, this is a misconception. Although they have publicised Third World issues in Western social policy circles, this review of the literature will show that research into the social policies of the developing countries has been undertaken by various social scientists for a number of years. It will reveal also that this literature is now extensive, comprising a substantive body of knowledge. Publications on the subject range considerably in complexity: while some cover only one social service, others report on a variety of welfare institutions or even the 'welfare systems' of developing countries. While some deal with only one country, others cover a variety of countries or even the Third World category as a whole. It would seem, therefore, that ignorance of this literature among Western social policy investigators is a serious oversight.

It is fair to point out, however, that a good deal of this literature is not readily available or accessible in Western social policy circles. Indeed, only a limited amount of Third World social policy research is published in Western social policy or social work journals or by Western publishing houses that specialise in the production of social policy titles. Obviously, Western editors will give preference to issues that they believe to be pertinent to their own societies and of interest to their Western readers. Third World topics are often regarded as exotic, having limited appeal. However, this attitude betrays an ignorance of the fact that Western social policy journals and textbooks are circulated internationally and widely prescribed at schools of social work and those academic departments that teach social policy in the Third World. While understandable, it has facilitated the uncritical assimilation of Western approaches among social policy investigators in the developing countries.

Another reason for an ignorance of much Third World social policy research among Western social policy investigators is the disciplinary diversity of this research. Unlike Britain, where the institutionalisation of social policy as an academic subject provides a focus for studies of the country's welfare system, Third World social policy research is pursued by a variety of academic disciplines which have an interest in Third World issues. Although studies of social policy in the industrial countries are also undertaken by investigators from different disciplines, the tendency is more marked in the Third World social policy field. The realisation that the problems of underdevelopment are fundamentally social in character and that social objectives should govern all forms of development planning, has stimulated a greater interest in Third World social policy issues among academic economists, sociologists and public administrators concerned with Third World studies at universities in both the developing and industrial nations. For similar reasons, interdisciplinary centres for development studies at these universities have also taken a greater interest in the field. Although social policy is still seriously neglected at both the interdisciplinary centres and the disciplinary departments, more research is being undertaken in the field. However, much of this work is published not through the conventional social policy media but in development studies journals or in books produced by firms that specialise in the publication of titles in development studies. Since Western social policy investigators, like other social scientists, tend primarily to peruse the literature sources of their own subject, much Third World social policy research that is published else-where escapes their attention. Just one example of this problem is the work of Mesa-Lago (1978) and Malloy (1979), two political scientists at the Center for Latin American Studies at the University of Pittsburgh who have inves-tigated social security systems in Latin America. Although their studies are of theoretical significance to social policy, they have attracted more attention from political scientists than Western social policy investigators.

Another problem is that social policy as an academic subject is relatively underdeveloped in the Third World. Relatively few universities in the developing countries have departments of social administration such as those which exist in Britain and often the subject is taught at schools of social work or at departments of sociology as an ancillary topic. Social policy research, undertaken from the perspec-tive of social administration, is pursued by a relatively small number of investigators in the Third World. Many of them are social work teachers at Third World universities who have taken a specialist interest in the subject. While their work conforms to the approach adopted by social policy investigators in the West, it tends to focus on 'welfare' policy issues, seeking to document and enquire into social work and social security services in the developing countries to the exclusion of broader issues.

Similarly, very few American or British centres for social policy research have developed a special interest in Third World issues, and with one or two exceptions research of this type is undertaken by individuals working within academic departments concerned exclusively with Western social policy teaching. The major exceptions are the specialist courses for social administrators and social planners from developing countries which are offered by British universities such as the London School of Economics and the University College of Swansea in Wales. Both have taught courses of this type for many years. As Mair (1944) reported, the first social administrators from the British colonies to be trained with the help of British aid resources began their studies at the London School of Economics in October 1943. These courses were subsequently expanded and modified to take account of new approaches and to provide a training that fused the British social administration tradition with the perspectives of development studies (Hardiman and Midgley, 1980). Although courses such as these provide a focus for Third World social policy research, the underdevelopment of the field in both the industrial and developing countries has meant that the amount of literature produced by social policy investigators is small in comparison with that generated by social scientists from other disciplines who are concerned with Third World social issues.

Another problem is that a good deal of social policy research undertaken by scholars in the developing countries is published locally and that relatively little of it receives international circulation. As noted earlier, it is difficult for Third World investigators to compete with Western colleagues when seeking to have their work accepted by Western social policy journals or by publishers of Western social policy books. Scholars in some developing countries have established their own journals and in countries such as Brazil, Egypt and India, local publishing firms are expanding their titles on social policy issues. But lacking access to Western markets, these books are seldom available in the West and only a few specialist libraries make efforts to obtain them. These difficulties are compounded by the fact that locally produced materials are often only available in local languages. Also, a good deal of social policy literature from the Third World is excessively descriptive and concerned with the operational details of particular projects. Published by Third World universities, research institutes and non-governmental organisations, often in mimeographed form, these materials are of comparatively little wider relevance, and understandably few libraries are willing to spend scarce resources to procure, classify and catalogue them routinely. These difficulties have relevance not only for scholars in the industrial countries wishing to broaden their subject by studying developments in social policy in the Third World but also for Third World social policy investigators interested in other developing countries both within their own regions and further afield.

In spite of these problems, a considerable amount of literature on Third World social policy is now available internationally. As indicated previously, much of this literature is to be found in journals and books in the development studies field. But increasingly, material is being published through literature sources that are more familiar to Western social policy investigators. Also readily accessible are the publications of government and, more significantly, of the international agencies such as the United Nations, World Bank, World Health Organisation and International Labour Office. Although often overlooked, these agencies have, as Hardiman and Midgley (1982a) suggested, undertaken more research into the social policies and social services of developing countries than academic investigators.

Those seeking to review the subject and order the available literature on Third World social policy are faced with a formidable task. The amount of research undertaken in the field is quite substantial, ranging over a wide number of topics and covering many different countries. There are, at one end of the spectrum, studies of Third World social policy that deal with only one social service such as housing or social security or education or medical care in one developing country (Stren, 1975; Hallen, 1967; Foster, 1965; Wilensky, 1976). Other studies examine a particular social service provision in a number of developing countries, particularly in regional groupings (Moumouni, 1968; Mouton, 1975), or otherwise they enquire into this social service in the broader context of the Third World as a whole

(D'Aeth, 1975; Murison and Lea; 1979, Wood and Rue, 1980; Midgley, 1984a). Other studies are not concerned with one particular social service but enquire into the 'welfare systems' of developing countries. These studies may focus on only one country (Dubey, 1973; Dixon, 1981) or they may examine the welfare systems of groups of countries (Mair, 1944; Simey, 1946), or at the most comprehensive level of enquiry, investigate trends in the Third World in general (Hardiman and Midgley, 1982a; MacPherson, 1982).

Obviously, different investigators will have different ideas on how studies of Third World social policy should be classified. Following a convention established by the international agencies, some will argue for a regional division of the material. Others will propose a classification based on the type of social service or welfare programme investigated. It is possible also to construct a typology of Third World social policy studies based on the numbers of provisions and countries covered. As shown already, this is feasible and could provide a comprehensive and convenient summary of the available research. However, a classification of this type would not offer insights into the qualitative features of different studies or discriminate between their various objectives. For this reason, the studies to be reviewed in this chapter will be classified into one of three familiar categories—the descriptive, normative and analytical—to examine their function and scope and hopefully to offer a more incisive and significant review. It is hoped also that students of comparative social policy will find this approach of heuristic value when examining the many other studies of welfare provisions in the developing world which are not discussed in this chapter.

In this regard, there is a case for extending the conventional boundaries of Western social policy research to include studies of welfare provisions such as drinking-water supplies, sanitation programmes, land reform measures and rural development schemes which are not, understandably, considered to be a part of social policy research in the industrial countries. But because these schemes have a profound impact on people's welfare in the Third World, they should, as Hardiman and Midgley (1982a) argued, form an integral part of Third World social policy studies. However, to keep the subject within manageable limits, this review will concentrate largely on the major social services. They are generally accepted by most authorities to form the central core of social policy's subject matter. It is obviously also simpler to introduce Western readers to the field if its subject matter is limited to broadly recognisable and familiar categories. Apart from focusing on the major social services, this review will be primarily concerned with studies that have been published in book form and that are reasonably accessible internationally. Journal articles, official reports and mimeographed material will be referred to only if they have particular merit or relevance to the subject. Although there are studies that do not fit easily into the three major categories of the typology, and some that span all of them, it is hoped that the classification presented in this chapter will summarise what is a diverse and complex but nevertheless interesting body of research.

DESCRIPTIVE ACCOUNTS OF THIRD WORLD SOCIAL SERVICES

Descriptive social policy research is undertaken by social policy investigators in order to document the historical development and present-day functioning of welfare institutions. The descriptive approach has played an important role in the development of the subject. In Britain, for example, a good deal of the literature of social administration offers descriptive commentaries on the workings of the British welfare state, examining the legislative bases, organisational features and major benefits provided by the social services. Although writers such as Pinker (1971) have been critical of the emphasis given to descriptive research in British social administration, it has provided a factual basis for the emergence of concepts and theories in the field. Indeed, its use has been defended by a number of authors who have argued that the theoretical development of social policy must be preceded by a thorough documentation of existing provisions. This notion is articulated as a rationale for the comparative case studies which feature prominently in Rodger's *et al.* (1979) examination of the social services of four Western countries. These 'constructive descriptions', the authors suggest, provide a sound basis for asking questions of wider theoretical significance.

The descriptive approach has been equally popular in Third World social policy research. As in Britain, most early accounts of the social services in the developing countries were essentially descriptive. One of the first of these was Blunt's (1938) review of the British colonial social services in India. Another early commentary by Mair (1944) offered a descriptive review of education, labour, health and social welfare services in various British colonial territories. Unlike Blunt's and other early accounts, this study synthesised a good deal of information pertaining to various colonies. Since the publication of these seminal studies, a large number of descriptive reviews have been undertaken, and there is every indication that they remain popular. At the time of writing, an extensive study of Nigeria's social services had just become available (Onokerhoraye, 1984).

Descriptive accounts of Third World social welfare institutions employ various criteria to structure their material. One of these, which is commonly used, is chronology. In this approach, descriptive narrative is phrased as historiography. Tracing the development of the social services in some detail, this type of study then reviews present-day provisions but generally not in any great detail. A good example is Landa Jocano's (1980) account of the development of statutory social work services in the Philippines which covered child care, family welfare, social assistance and similar provisions. Beginning with a review of customary practices among the precolonial Filippino peoples, Landa Jocano showed how their ancient institutions were gradually displaced during Spanish colonial rule when a Latin conception of welfare which fostered the creation of charity hospitals, asylums and almshouses was introduced. Modern statutory programmes were first established by the Americans, who occupied the country from 1899 to 1947. It was during this period that social work services gradually emerged

under a central government authority to provide a variety
of programmes similar to those that had been established
in the United States and other Western, industrial countries.
Another example of the historico-descriptive approach is
Dixon's (1981) study of welfare services in China, which
contains a remarkable amount of detailed information about
a country which has only recently provided information of
any real significance about its welfare programmes to foreign
scholars. Taking account of the post-Mao changes, Dixon
scrutinised a large number of documentary sources to
provide a detailed historiography of the development of the
country's income maintenance and family welfare services
since 1949.

A second approach is more concerned with the present-
day organisational and procedural features of the social
services than their historical development. Although these
studies usually contain one or two introductory chapters
that summarise the historical growth of the social services,
they are primarily devoted to a descriptive exposition of the
services in operation at the time of writing, concentrating on
their administrative characteristics, resources, expenditures,
coverage and provisions. One example is Onokerhoraye's
(1984) study of Nigeria's social services, which was
mentioned earlier. Apart from reviewing the conventional
catalogue of social service provisions such as education,
health, housing and social work, the book deals with less
familiar topics, including transport, water supply,
recreational and employment services. Western readers may
be surprised to note that there are no references to social
security in the book. Although these schemes, which are of
considerable importance in Western social policy research,
do exist in Nigeria, they were probably not mentioned
because of their limited scope and coverage. The underdevelopment of social security is common to many other Third
World countries as well (Midgley, 1984a).

Another criterion that is sometimes used to organise
descriptive accounts of Third World social policy is legislation. In this approach, the material is presented by
describing various legislative enactments governing the
social services, and usually emphasis is placed on the admin-

istrative aspects of these provisions. Although most descriptive studies of the social services in developing countries are primarily concerned with statutory provisions, not all make explicit use of legislation to present and structure their material. Cumper's (1972) account of the social services of Jamaica is a good example of this approach. In this study, Cumper examined a variety of statutes, both historical and contemporary, to describe the country's welfare institutions.

There is a dearth of basic descriptive research into voluntary social services in developing countries. As was noted previously, most descriptive studies of Third World welfare institutions focus on statutory provisions. Apart from India, where several accounts of voluntary welfare activities have been published (Kulkarni, 1979), this is a much neglected field. Also neglected are studies of indigenous or traditional responses to need. Like the systems of occupational and fiscal welfare in the industrial countries that provide 'hidden' benefits, indigenous welfare institutions have been discussed by very few social policy investigators. Examples include commentaries on the potential role of indigenous provisions in the formulation of social security policies by Ijere (1966) and Gilbert (1976) and a consideration of the implications of indigenous Chinese culture for social work in a collection edited by Hodge (1980). There is an urgent need for more research of this kind. As Midgley (1984a) argued, Third World governments could usefully adapt indigenous welfare institutions and integrate them with statutory provisions to extend benefits to ordinary people.

Although descriptive studies provide a factual exposition of the historical development and contemporary features of the social services in various developing countries, they suffer from numerous inadequacies. Often their meticulous concern for detail makes dry reading, especially for readers from other countries who are more interested in general trends than lengthy documentary case histories and the minutiae of specific events. Although suitable for reference purposes and of obvious archival importance, these studies are seldom memorable. A related problem is that descriptive studies are often rendered obsolete by changing social, political and economic circumstances. This problem is frequently encountered by descriptive studies of Third World social welfare that provide limited historical information, preferring to describe provisions at the time of writing. A dramatic example of this is Prigmore's (1976) account of social work in Iran, which was published a few years before the collapse of the monarchy. Although political change in developing countries does not always result in a complete restructuring of social welfare programmes, the patterns of social work education and practice described in Prigmore's book have been radically modified by the Iranian revolution.

Another drawback is that descriptive studies seldom organise or present their material in ways that can be employed readily in the formulation of social policy theories. Because they lack an explicit conceptual basis, less satisfactory criteria such as chronology or statutory provisions are employed to structure the material. Consequently, these studies offer little scope for dealing with a number of questions of general theoretical relevance which arise when the social policies of developing countries are examined. Nor do they usually discuss the broader social, political or economic context in which the social services have emerged in different countries or consider the broader social forces that have contributed to the development of the social welfare institutions in the Third World. For example, in Landa Jocano's account of the history of social work services in the Philippines, the influence of American approaches on the development of the country's welfare services is not treated as being of wider significance but reported rather as routine fact. By failing to comment on the effects of colonialism in shaping domestic institutions, the author missed an obvious opportunity to enliven his descriptive commentary with observations of wider significance for the understanding of the emergence of social policy in developing countries.

Descriptive studies do occasionally touch on issues of general relevance, but usually references of this kind are fleeting or reserved for perfunctory introductory or concluding chapters. In several sections of Onokerhoraye's book where reasons for the maldistribution of Nigeria's social services are examined, reference is made to a variety of historical, economic and social factors that have influenced the allocation of social service resources. But these comments, which lift the book's narrative above the level of factual reporting, are not developed adequately to offer generalised insights of relevance to other developing societies.

Another limitation of the descriptive approach is its lack of normative relevance. Although references are sometimes made to the problems facing the social services in developing countries, most descriptive accounts do not seek to offer a critical evaluation of the services they describe. Most authors of descriptive studies are content to report on the social services of developing countries without assessing their effectiveness or impact on levels of welfare in the community. However, the intentionally dispassionate style adopted in many of these studies does not mean that their authors are neutral in their reporting. Indeed, by failing to adopt criteria for evaluation, they sometimes imply that the situation is entirely satisfactory. Many tend also to define the social services in ways that are ostensibly impartial but which in fact presuppose that the social services of developing countries serve the noblest of purposes.

In view of the fact that descriptive studies do meet a very real need for basic, factual information about the social services in developing countries, it is perhaps unfair to level these criticisms against them. Descriptive studies provide accounts of the history, organisation and functioning of the social services in developing countries which are useful not only to international social policy investigators wishing to know more about welfare institutions in different societies but to students in the Third World; they are, as Adler and Midgley (1984) observed, often badly informed about the welfare provisions of their own countries. Although there is considerable scope for improving the descriptive approach, it has an obvious role to play in documenting welfare phenomena and providing a factual basis for theoretical speculation.

THE NORMATIVE APPROACH IN THIRD WORLD SOCIAL POLICY

Normative social policy research transcends ostensibly detached descriptive commentaries by seeking to evaluate social welfare institutions or to apply social science knowledge to establish or modify existing provisions. Like the descriptive approach, normative enquiry has enjoyed much popularity in Western social policy circles; indeed, a great many studies of social policy in the industrial countries have been explicitly normative, commenting on the adequacy of social provisions in explicitly moral terms. This has attracted criticism from social scientists in other disciplines. Some have condemned the vocational character of social administration, arguing that universities should not be in the business of training welfare personnel. A more serious objection comes from those who espouse the ideal of scientific detachment. Ethical involvement in social issues, they argue, hinders the application of scientific principles to the analysis of social reality and the discovery of objective truth through the scientific method.

In his assessment of the subject of social administration, Pinker (1971) commented unfavourably on the unrestrained and uncritical use of the normative approach by social policy investigators. Although value commitment is an admirable feature of social policy research, it is often so permeated with ethical presupposition that analytical ideas are widely sacrificed. This, he suggested, has hindered social policy's primary academic task of explaining welfare phenomena in theoretical terms. However, Pinker drew a distinction between social policy work that clarifies causal associations between policy decisions and their consequences and that which seeks to organise knowledge to fit preconceived ideological preferences and the attainment of practical objectives. The latter, he suggested, is particularly liable to introduce unacceptable moral biases into the study of social policy.

Pinker's distinction between normative social policy research that evaluates the consequences of different social policy choices and that which seeks to meet particular administrative or operational objectives, may be adapted to categorise the large number of normative studies of Third World social policy that have been undertaken. Those studies that apply social policy knowledge for programmatic purposes to establish social service provisions or to modify them will be described as *advisory* normative studies in this review. Those that attempt to analyse social policies in order to assess their outcomes in terms of predefined criteria shall be designated as *evaluative* normative studies.

Advisory Studies
A good deal of advisory social policy research in the developing countries is undertaken at the specific request of official organisations. Although Third World governments are increasingly commissioning research studies of this kind, the international agencies are probably the major consumers of advisory social policy research. Among these are the United Nations and its specialist agencies such as the World Health Organisation and the International Labour Office. Advisory research is also commissioned by the governments of the industrial countries for aid purposes. Often, aid for social development programmes is only disbursed by these governments after appropriate advisory studies have been undertaken in the recipient country. International non-governmental organisations which collect funds in the industrial countries to finance social projects in the Third World are also making increasing use of advisory social policy research to determine the need for particular programmes and to formulate plans for their effective implementation and functioning.

Advisory social policy research is undertaken by investigators working in different settings. Social scientists employed at universities in the industrial countries have been major providers of this type of research, usually through undertaking short-term consultancy missions to developing countries. Although social scientists from local universities are sometimes used to advise on social development projects, this is still uncommon (Hardiman and Midgley, 1978). However, it is somewhat more common today for social scientists from Third World universities to be sent to other developing countries as advisers. This practice is being actively promoted by the international agencies to counteract the predominance of Western Europeans and North Americans in the provision of international expertise. Also becoming more common is the development of the social policy research capabilities of the national governments of Third World countries. The central planning ministries of many developing countries are now undertaking their own social policy research or commissioning studies from national departments of censuses or statistics. In addition, some social service ministries in the Third World have established their own research and planning units and are strengthening their social research potential. Commerical consultancy in the field is also expanding. Although commercial consultancy firms have conventionally been concerned with engineering, management, agricultural and economic projects, an increasing number are bidding for research contracts in social development.

Because of their specificity and involvement with particular social programmes in particular countries, advisory social policy studies rarely have wider interest. Occasionally, however, they do raise broader issues or attract international attention. Sometimes, advisory studies are specifically designed to have relevance for social planners in other developing countries, and sometimes attention is explicitly given to the question of transferability. Studies undertaken for the international agencies are often of this type. Examining a particular social service in a number of developing countries, these studies seek to make broader recommendations which can be implemented throughout the Third World.

One example of this approach is a World Health Organisation publication edited and compiled by Newell (1975). This study was designed to examine ways of expanding modern health-care provisions in the rural areas of developing countries where health provisions are limited. Presenting ten case studies of health programmes from different developing countries which had extended coverage in this way, Newell sought to identify the features that were common to all of them and that were, therefore, characteristic of a successful rural health-care strategy. Although different types of programmes were described in the book, all involved ordinary people in health programmes, employed paramedical staff, placed emphasis on low-cost primary health services and integrated curative, preventive and promotional health care functions. Elaborating on these common features, Newell attempted to formulate, in general terms, an appropriate strategy for the development of health programmes in rural areas that could be adopted elsewhere.

One advisory study that received a good deal of international attention was undertaken by Titmuss, Abel-Smith and Lynes (1961) in Mauritius. This investigation was commissioned by the British colonial authorities who were considering the introduction of a contributory social insurance scheme in the country. For various reasons, the numbers of people receiving public assistance had increased steadily during the 1950s. This had caused some concern in official circles and had prompted a more thorough investigation of the situation. Titmuss and his colleagues were invited to study the problem and make recommendations. The team visited Mauritius on several occasions during 1959 and 1960 and, after collecting a vast amount of information, presented their report at the end of 1960.

Although Titmuss and his colleagues were requested to advise on the introduction of social security in Mauritius, they were able to widen the terms of reference of the study to include an examination of the island's social services as a whole and a consideration of population growth which they perceived to be a major problem affecting levels of and access to welfare. With unrestrained population growth, they argued, the 'health, child welfare, education, housing and social security services will be confronted with demands which will soon outrun the resources available' (Titmuss *et al.*, 1961: 238). To deal with this problem, they proposed the adoption of a comprehensive policy that would integrate demographic, health and welfare considerations and result simultaneously in a reduction of fertility levels and an improvement in social services. Family-planning facilities should, they urged, be expanded together with health programmes and be provided free of charge as an integral part of modern medical care. Social security should also be expanded and, in addition to providing a range of conventional income benefits, should pay a standard family allowance of 15 rupees per month to all families with three children under 15 years of age. However, to counteract the potential pronatalist incentive of this proposal, they recommended that the allowance should not be increased for subsequent children and that it should not be paid if the mother was under 21 years of age. This Titmuss and his colleagues believed would encourage later childbearing and improve child spacing, both of which would have a positive effect on fertility on the island.

While the Titmuss Report is not unlike many other advisory studies undertaken in the Third World, it had a number of unusual features which partly accounted for its international circulation. One of these was its attempt to adapt Western social policy approaches to fit local conditions. By linking the modern social services with family-planning facilities, the study revealed an awareness of local realities not generally encountered elsewhere at the time. Another example of this sensitivity to local conditions was an imaginative recommendation that the proposed social security scheme should provide a fire-disaster benefit. Because many Mauritian homes were built of wood and straw, fires were a common occurrence. Although not covered by social insurance schemes in other countries, the team thought it right that this contingency should be catered for. The attempt to integrate family-planning, health, welfare and social security provisions through a comprehensive plan was another distinctive feature of this study. By formulating a holistic social planning strategy, Titmuss and his colleagues were well ahead of their contemporaries, many of whom were later to be criticised for promoting fragmented and sectorally exclusive social policies (United Nations, 1971).

Evaluative Studies
As was noted earlier, social policy research is often undertaken to examine the social policies or welfare provisions of

governments without seeking to make specific programmatic recommendations. Known as evaluative research, these studies are usually undertaken by academic investigators wishing to analyse the content of social policies and to assess their outcomes in terms of various criteria. They are not usually concerned with particular projects in particular countries but rather with comparative assessments of different approaches to social welfare and different styles of policy making. Of course, social policy research may be commissioned to assess particular projects or social programmes, but in this case they should be classed together with the advisory studies described earlier.

Evaluative studies frequently draw on knowledge in administrative and political science to examine the policy-making process, and often particular administrative and policy issues are linked together with wider social, political and economic realities. Because they attempt to examine policy strategies in general terms, evaluative studies do have a clear analytical function, but they should not be confused with the analytical studies reviewed in this typology. Evaluative studies fall into the normative category because they have clear implications for policy makers, and their normative content is explicit. By assessing the consequences of different policy options and determining whether social programmes meet declared objectives, these studies seek to inform social planners and to offer normative guidelines for the formulation of effective interventionist strategies.

One of the first evaluative studies of the social policies of Third World countries to attract attention in Western social policy circles was undertaken by Livingstone (1969), an administrative scientist involved in the training of public administrators from the developing world. In his study, Livingstone focused on education, health and social work services, describing their features and commenting on their shortcomings. In each case he concluded with a generalised discussion of how the inadequacies of these social services could be remedied. For example, reviewing trends in education, Livingstone noted that while educational provisions in the developing world had been greatly expanded by governments, they still faced many problems.

In many countries, the curriculum reflected Western educational approaches, with the result that Third World students often knew more about English poetry than the history or present circumstances of their own societies. Another problem was the mismatch between educational qualifications and employment opportunities. Although many more young people were attaining tertiary educational standards, many were disillusioned and frustrated because they were unable to find employment commensurate with their qualifications. Another problem was unequal access to educational facilities among different population groups. Although popular demand for the expansion of educational facilities could not be ignored, policy makers were often insensitive to the educational aspirations of rural communities. This attitude, which Livingstone described as a 'mandarin syndrome', had retarded the rate of educational expansion and resulted in an unbalanced distribution of access to educational provisions between urban and rural communities and higher and lower income groups.

These various problems, Livingstone suggested, could be remedied by adopting social policies that changed the curriculum emphasis and linked educational provisions to the economic requirements of developing countries. Apart from a need for more careful manpower planning and a change in educational content and methods, he advocated the adoption of policies that extended education to the illiterate, expanded provisions for adults and women in particular and introduced vocational skills in agriculture and industry into schools.

In addition to assessing specific social service provisions, Livingstone considered the various factors that had shaped the social policies of developing countries and discussed the policy instruments that governments had employed to formulate and implement social development programmes. While his account of the determinants of social policy digressed somewhat from the study's predominantly evaluative concerns, Livingstone's discussion of the instruments of social policy was essentially normative. These tools of social administration, which include legislation, planning, research and administration, are essential for the creation and effective functioning of the social services, but they are often deficient. By examining their inadequacies, social planners can identify likely remedies and bring about required improvements.

Another pioneering study is Apthorpe's (1970) edited collection of papers on the role of social planning in development planning; these were presented to a workshop held at the Institute of Development Studies at the University of Sussex in 1969. There was considerable interest in the subject at the time, both in academic and official circles, and it was hoped that the workshop would clarify many of the issues which had arisen out of the theory and practice of social planning. Although greater clarity was not always achieved, many of the contributors made incisive comments on the problems and constraints facing social planners in the major sectoral fields of social planning.

Since the publication of these seminal studies, a number of books about the social policies of the developing countries have been produced. Among the best known are an account of social planning in the Third World by Conyers (1982), MacPherson's (1982) critical assessment of Third World social policy and Hardiman and Midgley's (1982a) review of social policy and planning approaches in the developing world.

Of these authors, Conyers is most directly concerned with practical issues. Reviewing the emergence of social planning and its present features in the Third World, she sought to evaluate its role in national development planning, sectoral social planning and project planning, considering how the social planner's contribution may be improved.

While Conyers approached her subject matter from the perspective of administrative and planning science, MacPherson adopted the interdisciplinary, theoretical perspective of international structuralism to investigate the social policies of developing countries. Emphasising the influence of colonialism on the creation of the social services in the Third World, his assessment suggested that the continued subjugation of the Third World to the interests of the metropolitan countries had directly affected the quality and scope of social provisions, resulting in a haphazard and uneven distribution of welfare resources.

In their study, Hardiman and Midgley examined social policies in each of the major social service sectors (including health, education, housing and social work) and considered a number of social development topics not usually covered by Western social policy enquiry. These were population policy, rural development programmes and urban development services. In their discussion of different policy approaches in each sector, Hardiman and Midgley employed three criteria for evaluation which, they argued, were particularly suited as normative principles for social planning in the Third World. These were appropriateness, equity and participation. Appropriateness referred to the extent to which social policies were suited to the needs of developing countries and took account of local social, cultural and economic realities. The concept of equity connoted the distributive elements of social welfare and was used to examine whether resources were allocated on the basis of need. Participation referred to the involvement of ordinary people in the creation, implementation and management of the social services. Reviewing the development and present functioning of these services in the Third World, they concluded that they did not generally function in terms of these criteria. Social policies were heavily influenced by the colonial legacy and, because of their continued dependence on Western approaches, were often ludicrously inappropriate to the circumstances of Third World countries. Similarly, the social policies adopted by many developing countries discriminated blatantly against the poor and the rural majority in general, resulting in a markedly differentiated pattern of access to modern provisions among different sections of the community. They noted also that although the notion of popular participation had become fashionable in development circles, it did not characterise the social policies and social service programmes of developing countries. Instead, the social services were highly centralised, bureaucratic and unresponsive to local needs. If the criteria of appropriateness, equity and participation were to govern social policy making in the Third World in the future, substantial changes to established planning approaches would be required.

ANALYTICAL STUDIES OF THIRD WORLD SOCIAL POLICY

Unlike the normative approach, analytical studies do not seek to comment on existing social provisions in terms of evaluative criteria or to apply social policy knowledge to establish or modify social service programmes; rather, they seek to explain welfare phenomena in abstract, theoretical terms. These studies are important for the development of social policy as an academic subject. As Pinker (1971) argued, social policy must generate speculative accounts of events in the real world if it is to attain the status of a true social science. At present, much theorising in the field is moral rather than scientific. This emphasis, he suggested, must be changed, for 'the first function of any kind of scientific theory is not to criticise what exists or to "transcend" what exists but to help us distinguish correct from incorrect knowledge' (Pinker, 1971: 100).

Although writers such as Goldthorpe (1962) and Pinker (1971) observed that there was a dearth of generalised social science explanations of welfare phenomena, Carrier and Kendall (1973, 1977) showed that the literature on the subject had grown extensively over the years and that an impressive variety of conceptual accounts of the genesis and functioning of welfare institutions in the industrial countries now exists. These accounts invoke the theoretical perspectives of different social science disciplines such as sociology and political science and comprise both positivist and non-deterministic explanations. Also, different theories ranging from functionalism to neo-Marxism have been employed to explain the emergence and current features of welfare institutions in modern industrial society in conceptual terms (Mishra, 1977).

While there are exceptions, few investigators have attempted to formulate theoretical explanations of the emergence and functions of modern social services in the

Third World in ways that take account of the unique features of the developing societies. Instead, most analytical studies of Third World social policy have replicated the conceptual perspectives developed by Western social policy investigators, and in many cases they have done so superficially and uncritically.

For example, conceptual references to the factors that led to the emergence of modern statutory social provisions in the Third World are often made in passing as a cursory prelude to a more detailed descriptive or normative study. Many studies of this type make brief references to the underlying social, political and economic forces that facilitate the emergence of welfare institutions in the developing countries and, in doing so, they usually invoke deterministic explanations which have gained currency in Western social policy circles. One example of this in the Third World social policy literature is the frequent use of what Baker (1979) called the 'social conscience thesis'. Aptekar (1965) employed it in his cross-cultural review of social work, claiming that the profession emerged to give expression to deeply institutionalised, humanitarian concerns. These concerns, he argued, are found in all cultures and account for the rapid growth of social work throughout the world. However, Aptekar did not pause to examine the merits of this explanation and instead stated the contentious assertions of moral determinism as self-evident fact.

Another common practice among Third World social policy writers is to invoke technological determinism when accounting for the emergence of modern welfare institutions in the developing countries. In her detailed discussion of social security in the context of development, Cockburn (1960) observed, in passing, that social security schemes are established as an integral part of the process of industrialisation and modernisation. Because industrialisation weakens traditional forms of support, such as the extended family, modern statutory provisions evolve to prevent widespread destitution. Although the welfare-industrialisation hypothesis can, as Mishra (1977) argued, be used with some justification to explain the development of modern social services in the industrial countries, Cockburn produced no empirical evidence to substantiate its relevance to the Third World but instead accepted that the theory's inherent logic and plausibility had wider international relevance. Consequently, a variety of questions concerning the diversity of modern social security provisions in the developing countries and the unevenness of these provisions in different parts of the Third World remain unanswered.

Although cursory references to established explanatory theories are widely invoked by Third World social policy authors, it would be misleading to suggest that no systematic research has been undertaken to account conceptually for the development of modern welfare institutions in the Third World. But studies designed specifically to investigate the genesis of social policy in the developing countries and to offer generalised theoretical explanations of their origins are rare, and many are equally dependent on established theories. In these studies, existing explanations of the emergence of statutory provisions are examined in the context of the Third World to test their validity in a more sizeable empirical field. Among studies of this type are Rimlinger's (1968) assessment of the relevance of the welfare-industrialisation hypothesis to developing countries, Mesa Lago's (1978) examination of the application of pluralist explanations in the development of social security in Latin America and Malloy's (1979) alternative account, which used a corporatist model to explain the development of social security in the region.

There are few examples of analytical social policy research that explain the development of modern welfare institutions in the developing world in theoretical terms by employing constructs that allude specifically to events or conditions that are characteristic properties of the developing societies. There are, of course, numerous historico-descriptive studies which emphasise unique events in the histories of particular nations that have been relevant to the creation of their social services. But generalised explanations drawing on concepts and theories that have been formulated to analyse Third World reality are rare. A recent development which contributes towards this task is the emphasis being placed on diffusion processes in the genesis of Third World welfare institutions. In these accounts, diffusion is conceptualized as the transfer of welfare ideas and practices to the developing countries largely through the experience of colonialism and the perpetuation of dependency relationships in the post-colonial world. The relevance of these relationships was examined with reference to social work by Midgley (1981), who argued that Western social work theories and practices were being transmitted to the developing countries through a process of 'professional imperialism'. Soon afterwards, MacPherson (1982) showed how social service provisions in the Third World had been shaped by colonialism and how contemporary inequalities in access to welfare were a direct consequence of the dependency syndrome. Later, Midgley (1984b) offered a generalised overview of the diffusionist interpretation, drawing on examples from various Third World countries during both the colonial and post-colonial periods.

As this brief review suggests, analytical studies of Third World social policy are still poorly developed. There are, of course, many more studies than the few referred to here, and they deal with many more issues than can be properly examined in this brief review. Also, they have not been discussed here so as to avoid duplicating the material in the next chapter, which seeks to examine the analytical relevance of Third World social policy research for the subject as a whole.

4 Theoretical Implications of Third World Social Policy Research

Although the study of social policy is a comparatively new academic enterprise, it has identified a distinctive subject matter, applied a variety of research methodologies to investigate welfare phenomena and generated a corpus of concepts, models and theories. However, as is generally recognised, social policy has not attained the same degree of academic formalisation and theoretical sophistication as the older social science disciplines.

Social policy's academic achievements have been assessed by a number of writers (Goldthorpe, 1962; Pinker, 1971; Mishra, 1977), and although they are correct in drawing attention to the subject's theoretical underdevelopment, they tend to overstate the case. While it is true that social policy's concepts, hypotheses and theories are inadequately standardised and systematised, it cannot be argued that research in the subject is primarily atheoretical. The conceptual images that were previously implicit in the writings of the founders of social policy have been formulated into a coherent body of normative theory that offers scope for organising key concepts. Also articulated are the social policy implications of major theoretical perspectives in the social sciences, such as functionalism, Marxism and pluralism.

However, it is fair to claim that social policy's theoretical knowledge has been abstracted from an analysis of a few industrial countries and that its relevance to other societies remains untested. For example, until the 1970s, social policy investigators in Britain had made few attempts to examine the applicability of their generalisations about the British welfare state to other nations. Pinker observed in 1971 that very little comparative research had been undertaken in British social administration and that the subject remained 'stubbornly resistant to comparative treatment'. (Pinker, 1971: 48). While a variety of concepts had been formulated and employed in British social policy research, they had not been widely tested in other societies.

Although attempts have now been made by investigators such as Rodgers *et al.* (1979) and Higgins (1981) to examine social policy concepts and theories in a wider context, the 140 or so countries that are conventionally classified as comprising the Third World are seldom referred to. Comparative social policy's focus on a particular group of nation states, located chiefly in Europe and North America, remains a major impediment to the theoretical development of the subject. As was argued in the Introduction to this book, social policy, like the other social sciences, can only lay legitimate claim to scientific status if its theories transcend particular societal realities and explain social phenomena in universal conceptual terms.

This chapter seeks to contribute to the attainment of this goal in two ways. First, it considers whether a number of theoretical propositions formulated by Western social policy investigators to explain welfare phenomena in the industrial countries can be substantiated in the wider empirical context of the Third World. Its second objective is to bring to the attention of Western social policy investigators a number of propositions generated by Third World social policy studies that may have theoretical implications for social policy investigators in the industrial countries. Although it was shown in the last chapter that theoretical enquiry in Third World social policy has been largely dependent on Western analytical ideas, some investigators have sought to formulate a body of knowledge based on a proper appreciation of the conditions of underdevelopment. Although still in its infancy, this type of research has produced constructs that require testing in the industrial countries to determine whether they have wider relevance. In this two-way exchange of conceptual information, the first tentative steps towards the formulation of a truly global perspective in social policy may be taken.

It is, of course, impossible in this brief chapter to examine the whole corpus of Western social policy theory in the Third World context. It is equally beyond its scope to discuss the relevance of all Third World social policy propositions to the industrial countries. But a number of theoretical issues which are particularly suited to this type of treatment may be examined to demonstrate the need for a broader approach in comparative social policy. But first, a brief discussion of the role of theory in social policy is required.

THE ROLE OF THEORY IN SOCIAL POLICY

A good deal has been written over the years about the nature of social science enquiry, with the result that a substantive body of meta-theory has now accumulated. Speculation about the methodologies of the social sciences not only continues today but is accorded increasing importance. Indeed, epistemological issues are almost as widely discussed as are aetiological findings. But while epistemological reflection on the nature of social science investigation has clarified many issues, it has also demonstrated that the production of social science knowledge is a complex task and that those who seek to comprehend and explain the social world face many difficulties. Methodologies that were once taken for granted are now recognised to be problematical, and the idea that the social sciences can establish a substantive body of objective knowledge is no longer accepted with certainty.

Discussion about the role of theory in the social sciences has featured prominently in epistemological debates. But this has not resolved disagreements about the nature and scope of theory. For example, the problem of empiricism versus *a priori* explanation remains contentious. While commonplace wisdom prescribes a healthy integration of factual research with theoretical speculation, these activities are still pursued separately in many social sciences and are still often taught separately to students as distinct sub-specialisms. In sociology, for example, social research methods are regarded as a separate subject from social theory, while in economics, political economy and econometrics are treated as distinctive fields. Empirical investigators and theoreticians are not always convinced about the importance of each other's work, and at different periods in the history of the social sciences, they have engaged in bitter controversies.

There are disagreements also about what constitutes theory in the social sciences. Although many social scientists have constructed models which conceptualise observable structures or patterns in the social world, they have been criticised for presenting little more than jargon-laden idiographic images of their subject matter. While critics of 'model building' in the social sciences argue that theory is distinguished by its attempts to analyse and reveal the complex causal interactions that take place in the real world, its defenders maintain that it is perfectly acceptable for theoreticians to be engaged in the production of conceptual schema that organise and interpret reality without offering aetiological insights.

Another example of agreement about the nature of theory in the social sciences concerns the notion of paradigm. Although this term is used in the natural sciences to connote an all embracing and universally accepted theoretical framework within which routine scientific investigation can be pursued, its use in the social sciences is not standardised. Some use the term loosely to connote any theory, while others employ it to refer to particularly popular theories or to 'grand theories' that offer competing perspectives on reality.

In the social sciences, the role of theory in explaining reality is complicated by the personal views of theoreticians whose ideas, knowledge and beliefs cannot be extricated from the subject of their enquiry. However objective they may endeavour to be, their perceptions of reality are invariably clouded by subjective experience. This problem is recognised in the distinction which is often made between analytical and normative theory. As was shown in the last chapter, analytical theory seeks to explain reality without making moral judgements or offering prescriptions for modifying reality. Normative theory, on the other hand, seeks to evaluate events and to formulate a coherent set of principles that will structure action. By distinguishing between these different types of theory, it is argued that social scientists may be aware of the subjective and distorting influences of personal experience. However, the distinction between normative and analytical theory is difficult to maintain in practice. Cognitive constructions may purport to be ethically neutral but often contain implicit value assumptions or reflect unconscious moral, political or cultural preferences.

These and various other epistemological disagreements about the role of theory in the social sciences occur also in the academic subject of social policy. There are arguments about the proper balance between empirical research and theoretical speculation, debates about what constitutes theory in the subject, and controversies about whether normative and analytical perspectives can be separated. In this regard, it is worth emphasising that many problems of theory that are thought to characterise social policy are encountered in the other social sciences as well. The problem of theoretical fragmentation and the absence of a coherent paradigm for structuring research is a feature of all types of social science enquiry. Similarly, the failure to examine propositions in a wider international context is certainly not confined to social policy: the problem of 'conceptual imperialism' characterises sociological, political science and economic research in many Third World countries. The problem of normative bias plagues the other social sciences as well, but it is often not recognised. It is difficult to see why social policy should be accused of ideological prejudice while Parsonian functionalism in sociology and contemporary monetarism in economics are regarded as scientific explanations.

Nevertheless, it must be recognised that some problems are particularly acute in social policy. Although the subject's theoretical underdevelopment has been overemphasised by some writers, the theoretical achievements of social policy enquiry do lag behind those of most other social sciences.

Also, the question of ethics is particularly problematical in social policy.

Problems of theoretical refinement occur at the levels of both conceptual formulation and theory-building in social policy. In their efforts to generate theoretical propositions, social policy investigators employ a variety of concepts as units for conceptual construction. These are used to generate both small-scale hypotheses as well as more substantive explanatory schema that offer comprehensive insights into welfare phenomena. Although social policy researchers previously used few concepts, Forder (1974) and Higgins (1981) have shown that theoretical formulation has developed rapidly. Also, while a number of concepts ranging from 'redistribution' to 'stigma' have been borrowed from other social sciences, social policy investigators have now formulated a number of concepts that allude to categories of phenomena that are particularly well suited to social policy analysis.

On the other hand, social administrators have formulated few explanatory theories of social policy and have tended to produce theories of the classificatory kind. As was shown previously, these theories which conceptualise welfare phenomena and order concepts into coherent structures or models without seeking to identify causal relationships, have been criticised by epistemologists for being pseudo-theories that do little more than translate particular concrete situations into abstract terms. The real purpose of theory, they argue, is to identify durable patterns of causal links over time and predict that certain events will occur under certain conditions. Social policy, they claim, has failed to produce a substantive body of theory of this kind, relying instead on conceptual descriptions of different types of welfare systems.

It is not correct to claim, however, that there are no explanatory theories in social policy. Indeed, a variety of theoretical accounts of the factors responsible for the development of welfare states have been formulated. But these theories are largely derived from sociology and political science, and they are sometimes accused of being teleological rather than explanatory. Functional theories are particularly open to this type of criticism. The fact that a welfare institution has a function in society, does not, the critics argue, explain its existence.

Because of its subject matter, the possibility of achieving a high degree of ethical detachment in social policy is limited. Also, since many social policy investigators are committed to values which cannot be readily separated from their understanding of the world, their writings are permeated with normative propositions. This difficulty is amply illustrated by their attempts to construct analytical models of social policy. Although these models purport to explain different approaches to welfare, inherent moral elements in their subject matter often frustrate the ideal of scientific detachment.

In spite of these problems, theory plays a crucial role in the study of social policy. Theory is needed not only to conceptualise reality but to communicate ideas in ways that can be comprehended readily. Studies of particular events and of causal links, however detailed and thorough, are of limited value unless translated into a widely used conceptual language. Theory not only facilitates the task of social policy enquiry but is an essential element in the efforts of social policy investigators to comprehend the real world. It is in this regard that the universality of theory is important. The challenge facing social policy research is to generate a body of theoretical knowledge that internationalises the language of ideas and conceptualises significant welfare phenomena in global terms.

TESTING SOCIAL POLICY PROPOSITIONS IN THE THIRD WORLD

These and other problems of theory will be kept in mind in the subsequent discussion, where representative examples of classificatory and explanatory theories will be discussed with reference to the Third World. An example of the classificatory approach is the models of welfare schema developed by Wilensky and Lebeaux (1965) to distinguish between different conceptions of social policy in the United

States. Their dichotomy, which makes a distinction between residual and institutional social policies, has been widely discussed with reference to the industrial countries and is today accepted as a classificatory theory of considerable value in the comprehension of welfare institutions. The explanatory approach is discussed with reference to a variety of propositions about the origins and functions of welfare institutions in modern society. As various reviewers (Carrier and Kendall, 1973, 1977; Mishra, 1977) have shown, these theories have been developed by Western investigators to explain why statutory social provisions have expanded so rapidly and now feature so prominently in the industrial countries. Both the classificatory and explanatory approaches are of illustrative value in examining the usefulness of Western social policy theory in the Third World.

Models of Welfare
Models are primary examples of the classificatory technique in social science theorising. They are relatively stable generalised images that permit social scientists to organise phenomena into systematic conceptual schema and to comprehend reality. Unlike explanatory theories, models do not usually provide answers to specific questions. Instead, they serve as abstract representations of perceived structures, systems of patterns in the real world. They do, however, provide a framework within which different propositions may be examined. But unlike explanatory theories, which can be empirically invalidated, models are not readily subject to experimental refutation. Models are not normally 'proved' or 'disproved' in the experimental sense but are regarded instead as being helpful or misleading.

Probably the best-known model in social policy was constructed by Wilensky and Lebeaux (1965) in their study of the impact of industrialisation on demand for social welfare services in the United States. To aid their analysis, these researchers identified two dominant 'conceptions' of social welfare in American society. The first, which they described as the residual approach, 'holds that social welfare institutions should come into play only when the normal structures of supply, the family and the market break down'

(Wilensky and Lebeaux, 1965: 138). The second, the institutional, 'sees welfare services as the normal first line functions of modern industrial society' (p. 138). In this latter conception, social welfare is accepted as a proper and legitimate system of services and provisions which caters for the population as a whole. In the former conception, welfare services are provided only for those who cannot provide for themselves. Although the authors believed that the residual attitude characterised much popular thinking about welfare in the United States at the time, they took the view that the institutional approach would gain wider support as the process of industrialisation continued.

Although Wilensky and Lebeaux did not use the term 'model' or go into any detail in articulating or generalising their ideas, their conceptual characterisation of prevalent attitudes towards welfare services in the United States has been employed by many social policy investigators. Their ideas have also been adopted to classify ideological approaches towards statutory welfare, to categorise different types of social services and even to differentiate between societies on the basis of their welfare systems.

While no rigorous empirical assessment of the usefulness of this model has been attempted, it has been discussed by a number of social policy commentators, and several reformulations have been proposed. Titmuss (1974) made extensive use of the Wilensky and Lebeaux schema and successfully integrated it with his earlier classification of 'selective' and 'universal' social services. Titmuss also added to the institutional model the notion of 'redistribution in command-over-resources-through-time' since, he argued, the institutional ideal is characterised not only by an emphasis on universalism but by a redistributive connotation. In addition to strengthening the conceptual basis of Wilensky and Lebeaux's dichotomy, Titmuss added a third category, the industrial achievement–performance model, which, he argued, ascribes a significant role for welfare institutions as adjuncts to the economy and 'holds that social needs should be met on the basis of merit, work performance and productivity' (p. 31). As Pinker (1971) observed, Titmuss employed the models of welfare schema in a highly normative way. By criticising the residual model for its conservative, anti-welfarist attitude and by linking the institutional model to socialism, Titmuss not only crystallised the ideological assumptions contained in the dichotomy but revealed his own moral preferences. As Pinker suggested, 'The normative element pervades Titmuss's approach but it derives from ethical rather than sociological theory' (Pinker, 1971: 100).

Pinker (1971, 1979) was critical of both the normative and analytical utility of the models of welfare dichotomy. The European welfare state, he argued, does not readily fit into either category. Emphasising the ideological features of the schema, Pinker suggested that the welfare state cannot be conceptualised as capitalist or socialist or as an illegitimate hybrid of the two. Rather, it should be treated as a distinctive entity with its own normative assumptions. Translating this idea into theoretical terms, he formulated a 'neo-Mercantilist' model of welfare which, he claimed, encapsulates the features of the mixed economy and the views of centrist thinkers such as Beveridge and Keynes.

Mishra (1977) associated the institutional model not with socialism but with liberal, social-democratic beliefs, which, he argued, provide an ideological basis for the European welfare state. The institutional model may be identified with liberal welfarism because it represents a compromise between socialist and capitalist ideology. A truly socialist model of welfare, he pointed out, is frankly adamant that welfare ideals cannot be realised within a capitalist system. The Wilensky and Lebeaux dichotomy, he suggested, requires extension to accommodate a third 'structuralist' model of welfare that represents a system of social provisions operating within a truly socialist society characterised by a socialist mode of production.

The fact that different scholars interpreted the Wilensky and Lebeaux model differently, associating the residual and institutional categories with different realities and recommending different reformulations, suggests that their dichotomy is of dubious value in comprehending welfare phenomena in the industrial world. Nevertheless, few social policy investigators have made a case for abandoning the schema, and many continue to believe that it is of general relevance and usefulness in classifying contemporary welfare phenomena. As Titmuss suggested, the models provide an 'ideological framework which may stimulate us to ask the significant questions and expose the significant choices' (Titmuss, 1974: 136).

How useful are the models of welfare approach in analysing social policies in the Third World? Although no systematic attempts have been made to test its validity and utility in the developing countries, the descriptive material presented in Part III of this book can help to answer this question.

There is historical evidence to support the contention that colonial social policies were characterised by a residual conception of social welfare. Colonial governments were primarily concerned with law and order and the maintenance of stable conditions for trade and agricultural and mineral exploitation. Social welfare objectives were low among their priorities and few welfare provisions were introduced. The colonial authorities were content to let the Church, missionaries and voluntary organisations cater for the social needs of their subjects, while their own interventions were kept to a minimum. Also, several authors (Hodge, 1973; Midgley, 1981; MacPherson, 1982) have argued that statutory programmes introduced into several colonies were compatible with wider European imperial interests and were often intended to protect the settler community. One example of this is the provision of public revenues for health programmes designed to control communicable diseases that afflicted Europeans and subjugated native populations alike.

It was for similar reasons that limited remedial social work services were introduced in many colonies during this century (Midgley, 1981). The growth of urban nuisances such as begging, juvenile delinquency, conspicuous destitution and prostitution occasioned a response from the colonial governments that sought to suppress these practices rather than ameliorate their root causes. Curative social work, residential care and poor-law type social assistance provisions (Midgley, 1984c) were highly compatible with the residual model. The notion that governments should take responsibility for promoting the welfare of all was not only incompatible with prevailing Victorian attitudes in the colonial community but also with the racism of colonial domination, which could not conceive of a non-paternalistic approach to welfare.

Although colonial welfare policies were characterised by a residual conception of social welfare, it must be recognised that some provisions which did not readily conform to the residual model were introduced by colonial governments. Although limited in scope, these extended coverage beyond conventional residual categories. In education, for example, British colonial attitudes began to change in the early decades of this century when state involvement expanded considerably (Mair, 1944). Although this was, as MacPherson (1982) revealed, motivated by a self-proclaimed 'civilising mission' and the need for a trained labour force, the expansion of statutory education was not compatible with residualist prescriptions. Similarly, as Midgley (1984a) observed, initial poor-law social security measures were gradually augmented by employer liability and other occupational provisions.

Nevertheless, residual ideas were widely accepted during the colonial era. They were also accepted and promoted by international development experts and economic planners in the immediate post-independence period. This was, as Midgley (1984d) argued, compatible with the prevailing development paradigm of modernisation, which stressed economic rather than social development goals. An obsession with economic growth and the supremacy of economic ideas in development circles relegated social welfare to a position of little importance. Although welfare ideas were regarded as worthy, social expenditures were disapproved of by the experts since they consumed scarce resources required for economic modernisation.

But while social planners in the newly independent developing countries operated within the modernisation approach and attempted to curb social expenditures, their ideas were slowly eroded by the domestic factors of nationalism and social demand. Missionary medicine, education and other social services had been widely accepted by ordinary people in the developing countries and, with independence, expectations for the expansion of these services increased. Modern medicine was proving its potency in treating communicable diseases, while Western education was perceived to be an effective mechanism for attaining salaried employment, particularly in the civil service of the new states. Although demands for the expansion of these services created pressures on political leaders that could not be ignored, many were not opposed to the rapid development of social welfare. Already before independence, many nationalist and 'socialist' movements had declared their intention to extend the social services to their people and, on coming to power, many gave priority to increasing health, education, housing and other social provisions. These developments were also compatible with the interests of the new Third World élites, who made extensive use of the rapidly expanding social provisions in the public sector. As shown in a previous chapter, these were concentrated in the towns catering primarily for the health, education and other needs of influential urban dwellers, neglecting the rural majority.

The demise of residualism in Third World social policy thinking was dramatic. In spite of the opposition of economic planners and foreign experts, social service facilities expanded rapidly. In international social welfare circles, where the residual approach had been generally accepted, its influence also declined. A revealing account of this development is provided in a United Nations report (1969) which showed how thinking within the organisation changed in the 1960s from a remedial to a developmental conception of social welfare.

In spite of rejecting the residual approach, few if any developing countries have adopted the institutional model. There is a good deal of evidence to show that social policies in the Third World do not serve a 'first line' function, redistribute resources on the basis of need or cater for the whole population. Access to social welfare is highly unequal, and because social policies have been copied from the industrial countries, they are largely inappropriate to local conditions.

Although there have been considerable gains in levels of welfare and a rapid expansion of social service facilities which now cater for many more people than ever before, Third World welfarism is not based on institutional social policy ideals. Instead, as Hard:man and Midgley (1981, 1982a, 1982b) argued, social policy approaches in the developing countries can best be conceptualised in terms of an incremental model in which existing provisions are expanded in an *ad hoc*, linear fashion and in which existing inequalities and inadequacies are perpetuated serving the interest of élite groups.

The contemporary features of Third World social policy suggest that the conventional models of welfare dichotomy in Western social policy do not readily fit the Third World. However, it cannot be claimed that these models are of no value in analysing welfare approaches in developing countries. It has been shown already that residual conceptions have been important in the past, and there is evidence of a recent resurgence of these ideas: the International Monetary Fund employs a residualist approach in its lending and 'conditionality' policies which has resulted in severe social expenditure cuts in countries receiving international credit. Similarly, some Third World governments, such as the military regime in Chile, have systematically implemented residual policies. On the other hand, universal health and social security programmes may also be found in the Third World. But it would be difficult to claim that the social welfare system of any Third World country is fundamentally institutional in nature. This is the case also in the so-called socialist nations of the world. In a pioneering study, Deacon (1983) found that social policies in three Third World socialist countries—China, Cuba and Mozambique—functioned primarily to serve the needs and interests of bureaucratic or state 'capitalist' ruling groups and to facilitate social cohesion and control. Also, instead of promoting institutional ideals, these policies were designed to respond to economic or demographic realities. While their social services conform more closely to institutional ideals than those of the East European countries, Deacon argued that the welfare systems of these countries could not be characterised as socialist. This finding has significance for those seeking to apply the models of welfare schema globally. While obviously helpful in analysing reality, ideal types rarely occur in the real world.

Theories of the Origins and Functions of Welfare Institutions

Research into the factors responsible for the rapid expansion of social welfare provisions in the industrial countries has attracted widespread interest. Many social scientists have recognised that the growth of statutory welfare in these societies is a development of considerable historical significance which requires generalised explanation.

Theoretical accounts of the development of social policy have been formulated chiefly by sociologists and political scientists. Although those working in the field of social administration have made a relatively minor contribution to this type of research, it is of obvious interest to them and several useful commentaries, which have critically assessed their value to social administration, have been published (Pinker, 1971; Carrier and Kendall, 1973, 1977; Mishra, 1977; Higgins, 1981).

Some of these theories are primarily historical, seeking to identify the social, economic and political factors that gave rise to the emergence of modern statutory welfare institutions. Others are less concerned with the historical dimension, focusing instead on their contemporary role in modern society. However, this distinction cannot always be sustained, since the historical and contemporary determinants identified by these theories are often interchangeable. This is particularly evident when functionalist methodologies are employed in studies of this kind. Explanations of the historical emergence of welfare institutions which rely on functional criteria can also be used to account for their contemporary purposes in society. Although there are differences in the extent to which theories of welfare employ a functionalist methodology, it will become clear that many reflect the long-established functionalist tradition in social science explanation.

Many theories of the origins and functions of welfare

institutions are also highly deterministic and, as Carrier and Kendall (1977) observed, they often reveal a fetish for the single cause. In these accounts, the development or functions of social provisions are often explained in terms of one overriding factor to the exclusion of a proper consideration of the many other likely determinants that interact in the real world to weave a complex network of causality.

A distinction may be made between explanations that are essentially empirical and those that typify the philosophical *a priori* approach which is popular in the social sciences. Studies in the former category include quantitative statistical analyses of the correlates of welfare provisions as well as qualitative enumerations of factors associated with particular developments. Examples of the *a priori* approach include abstract generalisations that attribute the development of welfare institutions to the rise of industrialisation and industrialism, or the differential political pressures of pluralism or the efforts of the state to exert social control over citizens or groups. Although the former factor-analytical explanations are not theoretical, in that they do not conceptualise perceived causal associations or structure them systematically into a coherent set of propositions, they do attempt to discover the determinants of welfare development and will be discussed here.

Statistical analyses of the correlates of 'welfare effort' have enjoyed considerable popularity in Western sociological and political science circles. Typically, studies of this kind quantify and associate a number of key economic, social, political or demographic variables which are thought to have relevance for the emergence and functioning of statutory social programmes. Political factors that have been found to correlate with welfare effort (as measured by social expenditure) include the ideological complexion of government, voting patterns and the degree of unionisation (Aaron, 1967; Pryor, 1968). One correlate identified by several investigators (Gordon, 1963; Aaron, 1967; Pryor, 1968) is 'programme age': countries that have long-established social welfare systems tend to expand them further to increase social expenditures. The level of economic development is another significant factor: several investigators

(Cutright, 1965; Aaron, 1967; Galenson, 1968) have shown that countries with higher national incomes allocate a greater proportion of public revenues to welfare. However, the importance of this factor has been questioned by others who have argued that geographic or demographic variables are equally if not more significant in understanding welfare effort. Kilby and Taira (1969) found, for example, that countries closest to the European continent had the highest welfare expenditures, while Wilensky (1975) concluded that the age of a population is a major determinant of welfare effort: countries with an older demographic structure spend more on the social services than countries with younger populations.

Some 'factor' studies do not rely on statistical techniques to account for the development of social policy but instead provide a qualitative assessment of factors that have been responsible for the emergence of welfare programmes in different societies. In some cases, several factors are systematically reviewed, while in others emphasis is given to one factor. An example of this latter approach is the frequent references which are made to institutionalised humanitarianism by Western writers when explaining the emergence of welfare provisions. Accounts of this kind usually attribute the emergence of modern social services to the benevolence of the state, which, it is argued, embodies the deeply felt humanitarian concerns of its citizens. Although this type of explanation was once very popular, it has been weakened by sustained criticism (Carrier and Kendall, 1973; Baker, 1979; Higgins, 1961). There are many examples of the former approach where the role of various factors in the development of social policy are explored. Among the best known, however, are studies by Rys (1964), who sought to enumerate the sociological factors responsible for the growth of social security and those of Heidenheimer *et al.* (1975), who reviewed the political determinants of public policy development in a number of industrial countries.

Although these studies often allude to established social science theories, they do not invoke them systematically. For example, few statistical studies of the economic correlates of welfare effort employ the constructs of the welfare-industrialisation hypothesis to interpret their findings. As was shown in the last chapter, this theory posits that statutory social service provisions emerge in response to the social problems created by industrialisation and the disintegration of traditional forms of support (Kerr *et al.*, 1973; Wilensky and Lebeaux, 1965; Rimlinger, 1971; Mishra, 1977). In this account, technological and structural changes rather than political choices or ideological preferences create the conditions for the emergence of modern social services. Also, because industrialisation introduces the same social changes and social needs in societies undergoing modernisation, it is argued that welfare provisions in different countries at the same level of industrial development have similar features. Rimlinger's (1971) historical research into countries of very different political traditions supported this conclusion. Modern social services, he found, emerge in liberal, paternalistic and collectivist ideological systems to provide for social needs through broadly similar forms of welfare intervention.

Although the welfare–industrialisation hypothesis is primarily a sociological construct, it has obvious relevance for political scientists seeking to understand the processes through which social changes create political pressures for the introduction of modern welfare provisions, and how, in turn, these are translated into political and policy decisions. These questions have stimulated a good deal of research into the role of pressure groups in the creation of statutory welfare in the industrial countries. Some of these studies have specifically employed pluralist conceptions of the political process to show how organised interest groups articulate demands for the introduction of modern social services (Hall *et al.*, 1975).

The notion of political pressure is contained also in explanations that accord importance to the role of the state in establishing welfare services for purposes of social and political control (Higgins, 1979). For example, it is argued that when faced with pressures from radicalised or potentially disruptive working-class groups which threaten the interests of ruling élites, the state introduces social service provisions to mollify revolutionary fervour and maintain the

status quo. Although this type of explanation is characteristic of Marxian or neo-Marxian theories of welfare, it also
has non-Marxist adherents (Piven and Cloward, 1971). But,
as various commentators (Pinker, 1971; Mishra, 1977;
Higgins, 1979) have shown, the 'conflict' perspective in
social welfare comprises a complex set of arguments which
are not always compatible or integrated into a coherent
theoretical explanation. The articulation of a neo-Marxian
theory of welfare by writers such as Gough (1979) and
Ginsburg (1979) has offered a more coherent account of the
role of the state in promoting welfare provisions in order to
control or manipulate subjugated classes and to further the
interests of capital. Nevertheless, these explanations share
many of the drawbacks of deterministic theories that rely
on functionalist methodologies to account for the emergence
of welfare institutions (Carrier and Kendall, 1973, 1977).

As was noted in the last chapter, some social scientists
have employed theoretical constructs when reviewing the
development of social policy in the Third World. But most
have done so superficially, referring to these theories
ephemerally and uncritically and often to add substance to
a descriptive or normative account. Although more rigorous
applications have been attempted, there are few studies of
this kind, and at present there is no generally accepted
theoretical view of the factors responsible for the rise of
welfarism in the Third World.

This is perhaps not surprising since the vast amount of
historical and contemporary information collected about the
social policies of the developing countries does not lend
unequivocal support for any one explanation. Historical
evidence can be produced to show that Third World governments have introduced modern social services for a great
variety of reasons and that they serve an equally varied
range of contemporary functions. Consequently, this information can be mobilised to support different theoretical
perspectives. Although this epistemological problem would
suggest that no viable explanations can be formulated, it
is, as Carrier and Kendall (1977) pointed out, possible to
compare a variety of accounts to gain wider insights and,

through a process of academic debate and an emerging consensus, to decide which are the most plausible.

While the various theories described previously all offer insights into the origins and functions of welfare in the Third World, most are implausible. Many rely on functional criteria and tend, therefore, to be teleological or otherwise excessively deterministic. In view of its complexity, it would be surprising if the emergence of social policy in the Third World could be reduced to any single determinant. Also, most accounts offer oversimplified interpretations of this very complex reality. For example, the fact that national income is positively correlated with social expenditures in the Third World (Fisher, 1968; Galenson, 1968) does not mean that economic development results magically in the creation of extensive social service provisions. This is equally true of the welfare–industrialisation hypothesis, which has been used by several commentators on Third World social policy to oversimplify the intricate political processes which operate to facilitate the emergence of welfare programmes. Since the decision to establish statutory social services is taken by the state, political factors play an obvious role in the development of modern welfare. Although the wider economic and technological environment may facilitate the taking of this decision, it nevertheless remains a political act. It is primarily for this reason that most satisfactory accounts of the origins and functions of welfare institutions in the Third World accord primary causal importance to political factors.

Of these accounts, the studies of Mesa-Lago (1978) and Malloy (1979) are among the most sophisticated. Both focused on social security in Latin America and both were primarily concerned with the political determinants of welfare. However, they produced very different explanations. Mesa-Lago argued that the development of social security in the region could best be explained in terms of a pluralist model. Different groups were able to exert differential pressures on the state which reflected their influence on the political process. It was for this reason that the most powerful groups, such as the military and civil service, were able to obtain social security coverage at a relatively early stage, while the economically weakest and least organised are still largely unprotected. A pluralist conception, Mesa-Lago, argued, also explains why the most powerful groups have the most generous and extensive schemes, while those for non-unionised labour are still very inadequate. Using Brazil as a case study, Malloy (1979) disagreed with Mesa-Lago's interpretation. The state does not, he suggested, respond passively to the pressures exerted on it by different pressure groups but usually takes the initiative for social welfare. Nor does the state function subserviently to the dictates of a ruling capitalist class, as some Marxist writers have claimed. This, he argued, is an oversimplified conception of the political process which fails to recognise the growth of the power of the state and the importance of state-centred political realities in modern societies. The development of social security can best be conceptualised, Malloy argued, in terms of a corporatist model in which political and administrative élites use social provisions to manipulate organised pressure groups and classes, to perpetuate established traditions of state-craft and to maintain the corporate structure.

Mesa-Lago and Malloy's studies are instructive not only for the insights they offer into the origins and functions of welfare institutions in developing societies but for illustrating the epistemological problem referred to earlier; namely, that methodological and detailed analyses of empirical data can yield quite different conceptual interpretations of reality. If this problem is encountered even when the type of provision and the historical, cultural, economic and political circumstances of the countries analysed are similar, the prospect of formulating a relatively manageable theoretical explanation of the origins and functions of welfare institutions in the Third World remains remote. Instead, it is likely that the complexity of this reality can only be encapsulated in a series of loose generalisations. Careful studies of the development of social policy in the industrial countries (Heidenheimer *et al.*, 1975; Hall *et al.*, 1975) have reached a similar conclusion showing that the exceedingly complex network of causality that facilitated the emergence of modern statutory welfare in Europe and

North America cannot be reduced to relatively simple propositions.

As will be shown in the next section, the problem of explanation is complicated even further by the fact that attempts to apply Western social policy theories in the developing countries have often overlooked factors that are particularly relevant to understanding of welfare phenomena in these societies. Although these phenomena require constructs that are suited to understanding Third World realities, they have not been widely used by Western social policy investigators studying social welfare in the Third World.

THIRD WORLD CONSTRUCTS AND SOCIAL POLICY

The finding that Western social policy models and theories do not adequately explain Third World welfare phenomena or take account of the particular realities of Third World social policy has different implications for social policy research. It may be argued that Western social policy constructs should be reformulated in the light of empirical evidence collected in the developing countries. Alternatively, it may be suggested that these theories should be limited to explaining events in the industrial countries and that quite different constructs are required to comprehend realities in the Third World. This latter view posits that social problems and welfare provisions in the industrial and developing countries are fundamentally different and that separate conceptual tools are required to analyse them.

As was shown in the first part of this book, there is ground for arguing that social needs and welfare responses in the developing countries differ from those of the industrial countries. It is the case also that certain welfare phenomena in the Third World are not properly conceptualised or comprehended by Western social sciences theories. Nor is it simply a matter of appropriate concepts. Social realities in the developing countries may be interpreted differently when viewed from different cultural and ideological viewpoints. For example, Western definitions of social problems often reflect liberal-humanist value assumptions which are not shared by millions of people in the developing societies. This is related to the epistemological question of how realities are perceived by different social scientists. It can be argued that a dependency on Western theory has weakened the originality of Third World scholars who might offer radically different interpretations of Third World realities if they were freed from the analytical predispositions of Western theory.

While there is a case for establishing a separate system of theory to comprehend Third World social policy, it has obvious disadvantages. It advocates theoretical *apartheid* and negates the idea of fostering a global perspective in the subject which has been repeatedly advocated in this book. There is a risk also that the differences which do exist between the developing and industrial countries may be exaggerated. For example, inequality exists in all societies, and although it may be expressed in different forms, criteria can be established to analyse this phenomenon in ways that are universally understood. There is also evidence to show that in spite of their differences, welfare provisions in different parts of the world do have common features.

It will be argued here that the findings of social policy research in the industrial and developing countries can be compared and cautiously integrated. Obviously, the problems arising from cultural and other differences must be recognised, and efforts must be made to control ethnocentric biases. Western social policy propositions must be tested more rigorously in the Third World, and at the same time, propositions arising from the study of Third World welfare must be examined with reference to the industrial countries. In this way, it may be possible to separate constructs that have particularistic application from those that have global relevance.

Social scientists concerned with development issues have employed a number of concepts that allude to Third World realities. While some have been borrowed from Western social science, others have been formulated specifically to deal with phenomena that are unique to the developing countries or the realities of underdevelopment. In this section, three interlinked sets of Third World constructs will be examined; they deal with the question of mass poverty and underdevelopment, ideological and cultural factors and the international dimension of the Third World experience. Each has direct relevance for understanding social policy in the developing countries and, it will be suggested, for the study of social policy in the industrial countries as well.

Underdevelopment and Social Welfare
The concept of underdevelopment is today widely used by social scientists to connote the persistence of mass poverty and its various manifestations in many countries in Africa, Asia and Central and South America. The statistical material reviewed earlier in this book provides dramatic evidence of the realities of mass poverty and deprivation, exploitation and oppression, hunger and disease and homelessness and landlessness that comprise the multifaceted reality of underdevelopment and characterise the life-styles of hundreds of millions of people in the modern world.

Different social scientists have emphasised different features of underdevelopment when seeking to analyse its nature and extent. Economists have placed obvious emphasis on the subsistence forms of production with low levels of output that characterise Third World economies and that perpetuate low levels of living. They have also been concerned with the formulation of normative prescriptions for growth and many have stressed the dynamic qualities of the modern sector and its potential for raising levels of living through massive capital investments in modern enterprises. Demographers have examined those aspects of underdevelopment that relate to population, showing that high fertility, a young age structure and a concentration of the population in rural areas are directly associated with the economic features of Third World societies. Sociologists and anthropologists have drawn attention to the structural and cultural aspects of underdevelopment, while political scientists have analysed the power relationships that characterise societies in mass poverty.

These analyses have spawned a plethora of theoretical

concepts. In addition, a number of interdisciplinary 'grand theories' or paradigms of development have emerged to order small-scale hypotheses and theories into coherent perspectives or cosmologies on underdevelopment. Three competing paradigms are now established in the corpus of social science development theory; they are modernisation, international structuralism and classical Marxism.

Unlike the other social sciences, the study of Third World social policy has not generated a significant number of propositions that deal specifically with the features of underdevelopment. Nevertheless, progress has been made in examining the 'factors' that are relevant to an understanding of how underdevelopment shapes social needs and social policies in the Third World. Progress has also been made in analysing the social policy implications of the major development paradigms.

Obviously, an understanding of the characteristics of underdevelopment can assist in analysing the nature of both social problems and social policy responses in the developing countries. In a pioneering review, Jones (1983) attempted to discuss just some of these factors, showing how mass poverty is a major determinant of welfare effort. The impoverishment of the majority of the Third World's peoples is not only manifested in massive social needs but limits the resources available to deal with them. The problem of poverty also raises the question of whether economic growth should be given priority over the efforts of governments to deal directly with its manifestations of hunger, squalor, disease and illiteracy.

The different development paradigms also offer insights into the nature of social needs and social policies in developing societies and, at the same time, provide different normative prescriptions for social planners. There is a congruence of modernisation theory and classical Marxism on the question of social needs since both regard underdevelopment and mass poverty in the Third World as an original state of backwardness. Midgley observed that modernisation theorists believe that 'primitive methods of production, an anachronistic culture, and apathetic personal disposition combine to maintain an archaic socio-economic system that perpetuates low levels of living' (Midgley, 1984: 83). As Palma (1981) revealed, classical Marxism takes a similar view: Marx wrote disparagingly about the 'backward regions' under colonial rule, arguing that it was only through imperialism that their archaic feudal structures could be transformed and levels of living raised. Offering a radically different interpretation, neo-Marxian dependency writers attribute mass poverty in the Third World to colonial domination. Writers such as Frank (1967) and Rodney (1972) claimed that once-prosperous regions were subjugated by European imperialism and, through the capitalist penetration of their economies, were systematically exploited and impoverished.

The different paradigms also provide different interpretations of the nature and scope of social policy in the developing countries. Again, modernisation theory and classical Marxism agree that non-interventionist strategies are compatible with the dynamics of development. This finds expression in modernisation theory in the notion of residualism which was described earlier and in the Marxian idea that liberal-populist egalitarianism hinders the emergence and consolidation of capitalist social formations in the developing countries, which are a necessary precondition for their eventual transition to socialism. While the insights of the dependency writers are depressingly pessimistic, they have inspired several analyses of social policy in the Third World. Various studies using the international-structuralist approach (Navarro, 1974; Doyal and Pennell, 1979; Midgley, 1981; MacPherson, 1982) have claimed that international and domestic dependency relationships have created social problems, siphoned away resources which could have been used to deal with these problems, and fostered a reliance on Western social policy approaches that not only replicates inappropriate measures but perpetuates entrenched interests and privileges.

Since the industrial countries are not characterised by a high incidence of subsistence poverty, with its associated social needs and economic, demographic and political features, it may appear that these Third World constructs do not have much relevance for European and American social policy. But it will be argued that Third World social policy research into underdevelopment does offer insights for social policy investigation in the West; indeed, some constructs generated by Third World social science research into underdevelopment have found application already. One example is Oscar Lewis's (1966) theory of the culture of poverty which was abstracted from studies of poor families in Mexico, Puerto Rico and elsewhere in Latin America, and which enjoyed some popularity in Britain and the United States in the 1970s. The grand theories which were formulated specifically to analyse Third World under-development also have relevance for the analysis of social policy in the industrial countries.

For example, the dependency paradigm, which has not been widely employed in the West, provides useful insights into spatial social policies. In the industrial countries there has been a growing interest in the territorial dimension of social policy, particularly in the urban areas but also in the formulation of regional development strategies. Policies designed to assist the 'deprived areas' have, however, tended to compartmentalize spatial categories separating deprived and prosperous entities in a way that is reminiscent of the theory of dualism in development studies. The dependency school rejects this notion arguing instead that central–peripheral relations extend into all spatial categories linking impoverished and prosperous areas into a single system. Its unitary model ends the compartmentalisation of the deprived–prosperous dichotomy and offers valuable insights for social planners concerned with these issues. The dependency model also offers a theoretical framework for analysing the flow of welfare in the industrial countries.

Conventionally, studies of the distribution of resources through the social services in these countries (Titmuss, 1968; Piachaud, 1979; Le Grand, 1982) have been largely atheoretical. MacPherson's (1982) application of structuralist ideas to examine the distribution of welfare in the developing countries points the way to the formulation of a more systematic conceptual schema for the interpretation of these trends in the West.

Culture, Ideology and Social Policy

Social science analyses of Third World development have neglected what may be loosely described as the cultural factor: shared attitudes, values, beliefs and institutionalised practices have not been given much attention. But this was not always the case. The first systematic social science accounts of developing societies were undertaken by anthropologists who were primarily concerned with the analysis of culture. In the post-independence period, as economics gained ascendancy in development studies, research into the cultural aspects of development waned. Although some sociologists and political scientists argued that cultural realities were an impediment to modernisation, their ideas were not given prominence in development circles and were, in any case, soon eclipsed by the dependency paradigm which gained widespread academic acceptance and paid almost no attention to culture. Dependency theorists tended to view culture as a relatively unimportant aspect of Third World reality. Since they argued that indigenous culture had been seriously weakened by colonialism and subjugated to the overriding interests of capital, this was not surprising. Even when faced with the reality of cultural differences between different ethnic groups, they tended to emphasise the integration rather than differentiation of Third World societies and took the view that ethnic conflicts were a mere manifestation of capitalist penetration. Similarly, while the notion of ideology permeated their writings, they oversimplified the concept and failed to recognise the cultural and populist roots of many political movements in the Third World.

In recent times, there has been a growing interest in the cultural dimension in development, and this has, to some extent, come about as the academic popularity of dependency theory has declined. Indeed, some critiques of the dependency school have argued that the theory itself derives not from socialism but rather from Third World nationalism and populism. Warren (1980) has characterised the dependency writers as bourgeois proponents of nationalist mythology whose views are highly compatible with the cultural attitudes of Third World leaders. More important, however, has been the recognition that powerful political forces in the developing societies are motivated by cultural beliefs. The Iranian revolution and violent conflicts between different cultural groups in countries as varied as Sri Lanka, Lebanon, Ethiopia and Nigeria, have not only demonstrated the political significance of cultural antagonism but its negative implications for development. As many economists and development planners realise, cultural conflicts are both socially and economically destructive.

Although more importance is now being accorded to cultural factors in development studies, social scientists have not formulated a coherent body of theory that encapsulates its various dimensions. Progress has been made, however, in the study of nationalism and ethnicity (Smith, 1979, 1981) and populism (Kitching, 1982). There is a growing interest in development anthropology which seeks not only to apply anthropological insights to development issues but to demonstrate the importance of cultural factors in development.

The cultural factor expresses itself in many different ways, and it is impossible to examine its relevance to the study of Third World social policy here in any detail. But two illustrative examples have been selected to show how, at very different levels of analysis, cultural factors are relevant to an understanding of Third World welfare. The first concerns the role of culture in meeting social needs, while the second examines the expression of cultural elements in the ideologies of nationalism and populism.

Any account of Third World social policy should pay attention to the institutionalised patterns of obligation and similar cultural practices that respond to the needs of dependent individuals and families. As was shown in a previous chapter, there are millions of needy people in the developing countries, including dependent children and the elderly, who rely on the institutionalised patterns of obligation in the extended family network for support.

Although these institutions have been mentioned in the writings of numerous social policy investigators, few systematic studies of indigenous welfare systems have been undertaken. Apart from idealised accounts of the congruence of Western social work ideals with traditional cultural values, which have been severely criticised by Midgley (1981), and normative proposals for the formalisation of traditional practices (Ijere, 1966; Gilbert, 1976; Midgley, 1984a), the subject has been seriously neglected. Research is urgently needed to document these practices, analyse their dynamics and functions and show how they relate to modern provisions. A proper understanding of these institutions would have obvious normative significance. It would also have relevance for the industrial countries. Titmuss's (1958) celebrated study of the social divisions of welfare stressed the importance of non-statutory provisions in meeting social needs but did not deal with non-formal practices. Third World social policy research in this field could illuminate the dynamics of non-formal welfare institutions and give deeper insights into the informal helping networks which are currently being researched by social policy investigators in the West (Froland *et al.*, 1981; Wenger, 1984).

Cultural factors expressed at the level of national ideology and political power are important for a proper understanding of the origins and present functions of modern welfare institutions in the Third World. Reference has previously been made to the significance of populist nationalism in the creation of modern statutory welfare in the developing countries. Many nationalist movements, struggling for political independence from colonial rule, committed themselves to the expansion of modern social service provisions on coming to power, and in many Third World countries the rapid development of the social services in the postcolonial era can be attributed partly to nationalist ideals. Certainly, no review of the origins of modern welfare institutions in the Third World can ignore this factor.

Nationalist sentiments continue to affect the present functioning of the welfare systems of developing countries. Although the concentration of social service facilities in urban areas serves the interests of urban élites, they are not averse to the expansion of social services in the rural areas. Indeed, much of the emphasis which is now being placed on primary health care, community schooling and other small-scale participatory social policy strategies is highly populist in character. The persistence of nationalist sentiments is related also to the limited access of ethnic minorities to modern social services. A dramatic example of this comes from Sri Lanka, which has long been regarded as a welfare leader among Third World nations. Jones revealed that in spite of the country's extensive social service provisions, the minority Tamilian community are denied various welfare benefits and are even required to carry 'distinctively coloured ration books which enable storekeepers to discriminate against them at time of food shortage' (Jones, 1983: 115). A similar example comes from Israel, where the Arab population are excluded from receiving many welfare benefits, even though their taxes are used to finance these provisions.

Nationalist and populist factors in the industrial countries have been almost entirely ignored in accounts of the development of social policy. And yet there is evidence to show that nationalist sentiments were significant in the expansion of the social services in countries such as Britain. Drawing on the work of Semmel (1960), Mishra (1977) showed how concern about the country's low standards of health and education in comparison with Germany created pressures for improvements. The ideal of a healthy, robust population was compatible not only with Britain's imperial status but with the then popular doctrines of Social Darwinism and racial supremacy. Similarly, Pinker observed that Beveridge's ideas reflected a keenly felt patriotism. Indeed, Beveridge argued that in adopting his proposals for social security, 'the British community and those in other lands who have inherited the British tradition have a vital service to render to human progress' (Pinker, 1979: 24). Although Pinker (1984) has also explored the role of populist ideas in social policy in Britain, these elements remain seriously neglected in Western social policy research. The Third World experience provides a good opportunity for examining the role of nationalism and populism in a wider context that can shed light on domestic developments.

Imperialism and the Diffusion of Welfare

A good deal of social policy research in the developing countries has drawn attention to the dependence of social policies in these countries on Western conceptions of welfare. As was shown in Chapter 2 of this book, modern health, education, housing, social work and social security services in many developing countries today reflect Western approaches and in many cases, replicate legislative, administrative and professional procedures employed in Europe and North America. Various investigators have commented on the normative implications of this uncritical adoption of alien welfare institutions, arguing that welfare programmes copied from the West have been largely inappropriate to local conditions, exacerbating the problems of unmet need.

Research of this kind has often employed the constructs of the international-structuralist dependency paradigm to conceptualise the mechanisms through which social policies in the Third World have been shaped by Western models. Midgley (1981) and MacPherson (1982) drew attention to the historical influence of imperialism and colonialism in the development of Third World social policy, and in a more recent publication Midgley (1984b) used the notion of diffusion as a conceptual and terminological shorthand for some of these processes.

These writers have stressed the importance of imperialism in creating the conditions for a dependence on Western social policy approaches. European imperial subjugation of indigenous culture fostered the attitude that ideas emanating from the metropole were superior and worthy of emulation. The acceptance of European languages, Christianity, Western modes of dress and similar tastes among many local élites, was curiously juxtaposed against their nationalism, which was later to rally popular support for political independence. Although it has been shown in a previous chapter that the colonial social services were poorly developed, the blending of nationalist populism with Westernisation fostered the replication of Western approaches in the subsequent expansion of the social services. Further examples of how imperialism created conditions conducive to a dependence on Western social policy approaches are provided by MacPherson (1982). The overriding emphasis on economic growth in colonial policy, the problem of urban bias, the creation of a centralised bureaucratic administration heavily dependent on an authoritarian legal system, the role of the missions in transmitting cultural beliefs and various other factors established structures that perpetuated the colonial legacy long after independence. Although international-structuralist writers had revealed the critical role of European imperialism in fostering social and economic underdevelopment, MacPherson argued that their ideas were equally useful in understanding social welfare problems and policies in the Third World. As he put it, 'Dependency and underdevelopment, with their roots in colonialism, are as important to an understanding of contemporary social policy as they are to the economic plight of the Third World' (MacPherson, 1982: 72).

Although the former European powers do not now determine the welfare policies of their erstwhile colonies, their continued influence should not be underestimated. Many continue to provide aid resources for social welfare, and usually its disbursement is contingent on accepting technical expertise from the donor nation. However, the role of new diffusionary influences in the contemporary world system must also be considered. Among these are the United States and the Soviet Union; although they were comparatively minor imperial powers in the nineteenth century, they now dominate world politics. Both Soviet and American approaches to social policy have found expression in their satellites, and particularly in Cuba and Chile.

Also relevant today is the role of the international agencies. Through their publications, foreign training programmes, expert advisory missions, international conferences and workshops, these organisations have been enormously influential in fostering the development of social policy in the Third World. Although they have not actively encouraged the replication of the welfare systems of any single industrial nation, their 'modern' or 'scientific' approaches to welfare have facilitated the continued transfer of inappropriate social policies to the developing countries. One of these 'modern' conceptions of social welfare is social work, which is not perceived by international civil servants and advisors to be an American welfare institution but a 'scientific' approach to social problems which has universal relevance. Midgley (1981) argued that the international agencies played a critical role in diffusing social work to the Third World, where its emphasis on psycho-social case work intervention is of limited value.

The constructs of imperialism and diffusion provide insights into the development of welfare institutions in the Third World which are often more useful than the deterministic theories described earlier. Research employing these constructs has shown that decisions to establish welfare provisions in the developing countries were often motivated by external pressures and that the perpetuation of these provisions today cannot readily be explained by using deterministic criteria. A good example is the vestigial perpetuation of colonial poor-law social assistance schemes in a number of developing countries, which are so badly funded and haphazardly administered that it would be difficult to claim that they serve any function at all (Midgley, 1984d).

Although it may seem that these constructs do not have much relevance to the industrial countries, there is evidence to show that the emergence of social service provisions in these societies has also been influenced by ideas from abroad (Rys, 1964; Hay, 1975; Higgins, 1981). But the role of diffusion as an explanatory variable in comprehending the development of social policy in the West has been seriously neglected. It is also seldom recognised that the emergence of welfare programmes in the Western industrial countries was facilitated by imperial influences. The power of Prussian-dominated Germany in the late nineteenth and early twentieth centuries helped to spread knowledge of Bismarck's social security innovations. Today the influence of American welfare approaches is also related to the country's global status. It is not surprising that the development of generic social work, community action and urban deprivation policies in Britain, as well as the adoption of culture of poverty and transmitted deprivation theories should have been so extensively influenced by American ideas.

Part III
Normative Relevance of Third World Social Policy

5 Restructuring Third World Social Policy

The enormity of the tasks facing social policy in the poor countries is such as to make the formulation and implementation of relevant policies of supreme importance. When considering the range of problems and issues to be dealt with we see conditions of extreme complexity on a huge scale. All the concerns which engage the attention of social policy in the rich countries are to be found in the poor countries. But the latter face further burdens of such magnitude that consideration of their needs and the responses to those needs is absolutely necessary. MacPherson (1983) has argued that the insularity of much Western work on social welfare has been deeply damaging; awareness of the realities of poverty and welfare in the greater part of the world is vital to any adequate consideration of welfare in the wealthy countries.

A number of problems may be seen as common to very many countries. Above all, there is mass poverty, and conditions of extreme deprivation in both urban and rural areas. This absolute poverty is found together with extreme inequality in living conditions, access to employment and the availability of services and social resources of all kinds. Although conditions have improved for many millions, across the world many millions more have become worse off with rapid social and economic change, population growth, urbanisation and the destruction of traditional systems of subsistence and support.

In all parts of the world, health remains a major concern; again there are massive inequalities in both health status and health services. Overall, most of the world is marked by low standards of health, with morbidity often increasing while mortality rates may fall. The issues of subsistence and health dominate discussion of basic needs—fundamental to social policy for the majority of the world's population.

Also fundamental is shelter, and we see that in virtually all countries of the world, housing is inadequate. More than that, in the rapidly growing towns and cities it is frequently not just inadequate but actually constitutes a major hazard to physical, mental and social health. This is increasingly so in rural areas also, where population pressure, restrictions on land-use and changes in economic and social patterns have deeply affected the provision and use of shelter in the context of local environments.

In education, for children and adults, the problems are enormous; massive expansion of formal education has been achieved but leaves enormous numbers illiterate and enormous numbers without skills they can use for employment. Formal education is failing to reach huge numbers of children and serves those it reaches very badly indeed.

Basic needs of subsistence, health, housing and education must be met, but so too must the need for useful employment and satisfactory social conditions, both equally part of any minimal level of living. These constitute social policy concerns of a vast scale, made infinitely more difficult when set in the context of societies marked not just by inequality but by *extreme* inequality. The drive for the satisfaction of basic needs for the majority of the population is the major task for social policy, but it has many others. As we have seen, communities have lost and continue to lose their capacities for self-provision of welfare. The loss is in resource capacity but is also in social capacity; the dynamics of 'modernisation' have displaced traditional modes. Together with the effects of rapid social change, this produces inevitable social consequences. Not just in urban areas—though most visibly there—societies are faced with the problems of child welfare, crime, family breakdown and individual suffering. Social policy must also be concerned with a host of specific welfare needs—of the old, the handicapped, those in need of social work skills and all those in need of care. As suggested earlier, the range of need is no less great in the poor countries than in the rich. Even greater is the harshness of the priorities that must be made and the cruelty of the dilemmas that are faced by those forced to deal with the enormity of need with resources which are very, very limited.

This of course is the overwhelming and crucially determining factor in all consideration of social policy in the Third World—the level of resources. We have seen earlier that available resources are, in comparison with the rich countries, so low as to make the nature of decision-making quite different; to force consideration of alternatives even against all the social policy imperatives. This is a theme we shall consider in this chapter: the emergence in the poor countries of the world of approaches to social policy which have begun to establish new forms and a new dynamic. But these advances are made in the most adverse circumstances and most often within a framework of organised welfare institutions which, as we have seen, acts to prevent the development of genuine welfare responses. The brief outlines of social policy issues which constitute the remainder of this chapter will illustrate and illuminate some of the constraints on social policy and the ways in which inappropriate policies are generated and supported. But they will also demonstrate more positive developments and in so doing identify common themes in new approaches to social policy and social welfare provision.

HEALTH

Health is fundamental to every child, woman and man, and affects every part of their lives. It is not a matter of curing diseases or even of preventing them. The right to health means not just the right to be free of disease but the right to physical, emotional and mental well-being. As a goal, and objective of development, health has a major place, and it is now recognised in social policy that just as health itself cannot be separated from political, economic and

cultural systems of societies, neither can health policies
(Abel-Smith and Leiserson, 1978).

Although conceptions such as these have come to the fore
in recent years and have come to provide the basis for major
shifts in approaches to health (as will be seen later), the
realities of sickness and pain, life and death for the vast
majority are still dominated by physical illness. Life expectancy has improved substantially in recent years but remains
very much lower in the poor countries than in the rich.
Similarly, infant and child mortality rates have fallen
throughout the world, in some regions and countries very
dramatically; but they still remain very high indeed and
stand testament to suffering and distress so great it cannot
be measured. Measures of death tell us a great deal, but
they do not measure the continual suffering from non-fatal
illness which affects such a large part of the world's population (MacPherson, 1982: 94–6). On all measures, of all
kinds, the extent of *ill-health* is vast, and must be a major
priority in any poor country (World Health Organisation,
1981b).

A fundamentally important feature of the patterns of
morbidity and mortality is that, just as there is considerable
variation between countries, so too is there very considerable variation *within* countries (Open University, 1985).
There are, above all, inequalities between social classes,
more extreme than any found in the rich nations. Closely
allied with those inequalities, and reflecting basic dimensions of development and underdevelopment are inequalities between urban and rural areas. Around the world, the
health of the rural majorities is very much worse than that
of the urban minorities, as measured in terms of death and
disease (World Bank, 1980, 1984). When more complex
and far-reaching notions of well-being are considered the
comparison becomes more difficult but does not undermine
this massive inequality within nations (Lipton, 1977). In
Papua New Guinea, for example, the infant mortality rate
was estimated at 72 per 1,000 in 1980. But the variation
within the country was from 35 per 1,000 in the area around
the capital to well over 100 per 1,000 in a number of rural
provinces. Within these provinces, particular communities

had infant mortality rates which were close to 200 per 1,000 (Bakker, 1984). This pattern is typical of predominantly rural poor countries—the majority (United Nations, 1981). Although there are very serious limitations on the avail- ability and reliability of data in many countries, the pattern of gross internal inequality is repeated everywhere (Golladay, 1980; World Bank, 1980; World Health Organis- ation, 1981a; 1982a).

Health Needs

It has long been recognised that the diseases of the developing countries are the diseases of poverty; lack of clean water, inadequate nutrition, population growth and poor environmental conditions provide the conditions for the common diseases to flourish (World Health Organis- ation, 1978, 1981b). Of course, there is considerable vari- ation between countries and again within countries in patterns of illness and disease, just as there is in patterns of mortality and morbidity. But it is accepted that the health conditions of *the poor majority* in the poor countries of the world are basically similar:

Their core disease pattern consists of the faecally related and air-borne diseases and malnutrition. These three disease groups account for the majority of deaths among the poorest people in developing countries. Malnutrition is the primary cause of death among children in the developing world and also a major contributor to the virulence of infec- tious diseases by impairing normal body responses to the disease, thereby reducing immunity levels [Benyoussef and Christian, 1977: 402].

Thus infectious diseases are the most important category in the poor countries; not predominantly diseases specific to particular parts of the world, although malaria is a major and growing problem, but diseases common to the whole world. Measles is an example.

Two million two hundred thousand children under 5 years old died of measles in 1980, according to WHO estimates, and in one African study measles was found to be the 'precipitating cause' in half the cases of hospitalisation for malnutrition (UNICEF, 1983: 42). Measles is quite obvi- ously not a 'tropical disease'; it is common in the rich countries but is rarely a cause of death in those countries. The appalling toll of suffering in the poor countries, and above all among children results from the destructive and pernicious alliance of malnutrition and infection which continually undermines health and makes children vulnerable to the ravages of further infection.

The World Health Organisation, and others, have attempted to estimate the number of cases of different types of disease on a world-wide basis. This is extremely difficult given the limitations of the data, but the predominance of malnutrition and a few major infectious diseases, in both mortality and disease prevalence is so stark that there can be no room for doubt as to what the major problems in the world really are. Walsh and Warren (1979), using WHO figures and published epidemiological studies, estimated the pattern of disease for Africa, Asia and Latin America. Table 5.1 shows their results. The impact of malnutrition can be seen, as can that of measles, already identified as a major threat to children.

But the most dramatic aspect of the figures presented here, and repeated in studies around the world, is the overwhelming significance of diarrhoeal diseases. These diseases, as can be seen, are responsible for an enormous proportion of the disease prevalence. Even with the inclusion of respiratory infections, excluded from the Walsh and Warren estimates, the enormous significance of diarrhoea remains (IDS Health Group, 1978; MacPherson, 1980; Morley, 1983; World Health Organisation, 1983a). Later in this chapter there is a more detailed discussion of this problem and responses to it; at this point its importance must be underlined and its relationship to other factors emphasised. More than 500 million children suffered diarrhoeal infection, three or four times a year. It is so common that it is seen as both a normal part of childhood, and indeed of adulthood too, where its effects are serious but not so often fatal. In Africa, Asia and Latin America in 1975 there were between 5 million–18 million deaths as a result of these attacks of diarrhoea. The diarrhoea and the deaths were the result of a number of factors acting

Table 5.1: *Proportions of mortality and disease prevalence of the major infectious diseases and malnutrition of Africa, Asia and Latin America, 1977–8*

Infection	Infections (000s/yr)	Deaths (000s/yr)
Diarrhoeas	3,000,000–5,000,000	5,000–10,000
Respiratory infections		4,000–5,000
Malaria	800,000	1,200
Measles	85,000	900
Schistosomiasis	200,000	500–1,000
Whooping cough	70,000	250–450
Tuberculosis	1,000,000	400
Neonatal tetanus	120–80	100–50
Diphtheria	40,000	50–60
Hookworm	700,000–900,000	50–60
South American trypanosomiasis	12,000	60
Onchocerciasis		
Skin disease	30,000	low
River blindness		20–50
Meningitis	150	30
Amebiasis	400,000	30
Ascariasis	800,000–1,000,000	20
Poliomyelitis	80,000	10–20
Typhoid	1000	25
Leishmaniasis	12,000	5
African trypanosomiasis	1,000	5
Leprosy		very low
Trichuriasis	500,000	low
Filariasis	250,000	low
Giardiasis	200,000	very low
Dengue	3,000–4,000	0.1
Malnutrition	5,000,000–800,000	2,000

Source: Adapted from Walsh and Warren, 1979.

together: contaminated water and food, inadequate nutrition and dehydration.

Children who are not well nourished will get diarrhoea more often, and its effects will be more severe—they will more often die than well-nourished children. But of course the diarrhoea itself adds to the effects of existing malnutrition and will begin to cause malnutrition where non existed. There is a cruel relationship between infection and the strength needed to fight it in which the victim is progressively weakened and made more vulnerable. Thus a great part of illness and suffering is the result of simple infections cruelly complicated by inadequate nutrition and contaminated water.

The massive significance of water supply and sanitation can also be seen in the prevalence and effects of intestinal parasites. Over 1 billion people, largely in the poor countries have worm infestations (World Bank, 1980). The commonest infestations are of hookworm and roundworm; again children are most vulnerable (Feacham, *et al.*, 1977). It is conditions such as these that determine the state of health of the vast majority.

The patterns of mortality and morbidity are now well known. Both are quite clearly the result of malnutrition, gastro-intestinal diseases, respiratory diseases, and vector-borne diseases. The knowledge needed to deal with them is widely available, they are relatively cheap to treat and to a great extent can be controlled by public health and health education initiatives if these are undertaken in concert with other appropriate actions: 'the health problems of developing countries can be controlled or treated with presently known technologies' (World Bank, 1980: 16). Despite mounting evidence that wealthier, largely urban minorities in poor countries are beginning to suffer the 'diseases of affluence'—especially heart disease—the mass of people do not.

Health Policies
The pattern of sickness and disease should determine the nature of policies and programmes. But for many years, the extremely limited resources of poor countries have been used to construct health services and to maintain health policies which have not reflected the needs of the majority (MacPherson, 1982). They have grown to reflect dominant social patterns and the imperatives of an approach to medicine and health dominated by Western concepts and values.

The pattern of health resources characteristic of the poor countries is one of very low levels of staffing and facilities marked by extremely uneven distribution. For the vast majority access to medical treatment remains slight and in many cases is non-existent. The bias is in favour of urban areas and areas where the formal cash economy is most advanced. In terms of approach, there remains considerable bias to treatment-centred institutional health care. Contemporary health policy issues have to be seen against a background of massive need, low resources, extreme inequality and an inappropriate pattern of established services (Gish, 1977, 1979; Doyal and Pennell, 1979).

The enormous impact of colonial patterns of medical care has been widely documented; so too has the continuing influence of outside forces on the health systems of the poor countries. This has been identified in medical training and the power of health professions internationally (Doyal and Pennell, 1979), the effects of aid (Hayter, 1971; Abel-Smith and Leiserson, 1978), the drug industry (Melrose, 1982; Muller, 1982; Rolt, 1985) and most pervasive and powerful of all in the attitudes and expectations of minorities within poor countries who have demanded and continue to demand 'Western-style' health facilities.

In both rich and poor countries, health care and services have been increasingly defined in terms of medicine and medical care rather than in terms of those activities and behaviours which actually produce health, or ill-health. Water, food, environment and life-style are known to be the major determinants of health, rather than the activities of the medical profession. Yet most countries devote huge and increasing sums to curative, high-technology medicine, which requires Western-style institutional and expensively trained personnel to administer. The poor countries, as we have seen, have patterns of need which demand relatively simple treatment programmes on a vast scale, and which are susceptible to prevention by public health measures. It is still the case that in three-quarters of the Third World, doctors work in urban areas where three-quarters of the health budgets are spent. But three-quarters of the people, and three-quarters of the ill-health, are in the rural areas.

The need for change has been long recognised; very many newly independent states in the 1960s made enormous efforts to improve health. There was expansion, but most often in the form developed under colonialism. Despite stated objectives, health allocations were still biased in favour of emerging élite and urban groups—'the rhetoric emphasised preventive and rural priorities at the same time that expenditures were overwhelmingly curative and urban' (Gish, 1979: 206). It was not until the 1970s that a radical shift began to take place in national approaches to health:

history and experience show that conventional health services organised along Western or other centralised lines, are unlikely to expand to meet the basic needs of all people . . . Clearly the time has come to take a fresh look at the world's priority health problems and at alternative approaches to their solution [Djukanovic and Mach, 1978: 7].

The Alma Ata Conference in 1978 officially launched the concept of 'Primary Health Care' (PHC), which was the expression of these alternative approaches to priority problems (World Health Organisation, 1978). The Declaration of Alma Ata stressed the 'existing gross inequality' in health status and access to services for health and argued for an approach to provision based on the notion of 'essential health care that is accessible, affordable and acceptable to everyone in the country'.

The definition of PHC adopted at Alma Ata has been taken up by very many countries since 1978 and has had an enormous impact on the content of national health plans and documents around the world (Morley *et al.*, 1983). The concept is revolutionary in its shift of attention away from medicine to health and the social production of health and ill-health. A part of the Alma Ata definition will illustrate its nature:

Primary Health Care:
2. addresses the main health problems in the community, providing promotive, preventive, curative and rehabilitative services accordingly;
3. includes at least: education concerning prevailing health problems and the methods of preventing and controlling them; promotion of food supply and proper nutrition; an adequate supply of safe water and basic sanitation; maternal and child health care, including family planning; immunisation against the major infectious diseases; prevention and control of locally endemic diseases; appropriate treatment of common diseases and injuries; and provision of essential drugs;
4. involves, in addition to health sector, all related sectors . . .

5. requires and promotes maximum community and individual self-reliance and participation . . .
6. . . . priority to those most in need;
7. relies . . . on health workers . . . as well as traditional practitioners . . . to respond to the expressed health needs of the community [World Health Organisation, 1978: VIII–IX].

It was therefore extremely clear in its statement of objectives and intentions. It was much less clear about the specific means by which those objectives might be met and those intentions realised. In 1979 Bennett, a leading authority, was cautiously optimistic about the prospects for the implementation of primary health care in practice. He did, however, identify a number of deficiencies in existing health systems and other obstacles which would need to be overcome (Bennett, 1979). Enthusiasm for the concept was high, and remains so, although not universal. A number of critics, for example Navarro, have pointed to the lack of analysis of fundamental socio-economic forces and constraints (Navarro, 1984). The proponents of PHC emphasise its applicability in any socio-political context, thus attempting to bypass the fundamental issues of underdevelopment and its consequences in very many states. This is clearly a major difficulty for PHC and for social welfare policy in general in poor countries. The extent to which significant and lasting change in the conditions of life of the mass of people can be achieved within the framework of existing social, economic and political conditions, and without radical restructuring of those conditions is a constant and vital question.

A number of commentators, more enthusiastic for the concept than Navarro, but with doubts regarding its implementation, have pointed to the importance of the context in which PHC operates (Gish, 1979, 1983; MacPherson, 1982; Rifkin, 1981, 1983; Segall, 1983). We have in health policy in the poor countries an extremely important example of the constraints which can prevent or pervert implementation of policies and programmes universally acknowledged to be the most appropriate.

It is not possible to take health practice out of its social political and economic context. The question which in practice faces those concerned with the quality of life of the mass of people is how much improvement can be made. There is no doubt that genuine primary health care can only be extensively developed if there are fundamental reforms of conventional health systems; this demands massive shifts in resource allocations, patterns of service and distributions of power within health systems. To be successful as an approach to health, PHC cannot be a matter of projects 'grafted on' to existing systems; the nature of those systems must change:

It must be stressed that the major obstacles to more just and efficient health care systems . . . are not the usually cited ones of limited resources, poor communications, or lack of technological knowledge and data but rather social systems that place a low value on the health needs of the poor [Gish, 1979: 209].

It is of course the case that the great majority of social systems continue to place a low value on the health needs of the poor, and in terms of fundamental change there can be little doubt that health is not simply, or even primarily, a matter of medical systems, but the product of the complex forces of development and underdevelopment.

But, even within that perspective, change is possible to a degree; improvement is possible to an extent; new approaches are possible; there are opportunities for local initiatives which truly express the principles of primary health care. National change has been found to be extremely difficult (Bossert, 1984; Vaughan *et al.*, 1984), but smaller-scale change is reported from communities around the world (Deuschle, 1982; Morley *et al.*, 1983; UNICEF, 1984).

Health and development is a vast and complex topic. Three examples will serve to illustrate some of that diversity.

National Progress in PHC: Benin
The West African state of Benin is among the very poorest countries of the world. It had an overall infant mortality rate of 150 per 1,000 (1981), and GNP of US $320 per capita (1981) and literacy rates of 40 per cent for men and 17 per cent for women (UNICEF, 1984: 182). According to Lachenmann (1982), Benin is particularly suitable as a case study in the implementation of PHC for two reasons. First,

the country has since 1977 pursued a basic-needs oriented health policy, emphasising preventive medicine for the masses, the integration of traditional medicine and the employment of voluntary village health workers. Second, the stated political intention is that the country should pursue 'an independent development strategy designed to improve the living conditions of the whole population under the slogan "Rely on your own forces" ' (Lachenmann, 1982: 102). The country has approximately $3 per capita available for annual health expenditure.

The stated strategy is clearly appropriate to the conditions and needs of the mass of people, but Lachenmann's account suggests that the health system has difficulty in putting the strategy into practice. There is a tendency to higher qualifications and specialisation among a small professional élite; health care institutions are not oriented to basic needs. The people have not been mobilised to help themselves and control their own health, but existing categories of paid health staff have been joined by a new group of unpaid voluntary health workers.

The strategy puts great emphasis on the rehabilitation of traditional medicine and its integration into the institutional health system, but in practice there are many difficulties due, it is felt, to 'the excessive emphasis placed on the pharmaceutical aspect and the "modern controls" to which traditional healers are subject' (Lachenmann, 1982: XII). Perhaps more significant still, it was found that the people even in remote areas had exaggerated expectations of the powers of modern medicine, which led them to neglect their own preventive activities and lose confidence in their own abilities.

The crucial relationships between health and its wider context are clear:

The most striking finding, which applies to more than just the health problem, is that *structural conditions prevent the potential for popular participation from developing* . . . 'unequal development' does not allow people to assume responsibility for their own health or to help themselves in the true sense . . . An intersectoral, politically enforced health policy is not being implemented because adequate material and technical support does not reach the grass-roots level, leading to despair in the

technical services and among the people they are trying to help [Lachen-
mann, 1982: XII, emphasis added].

Welfare institutions in Benin are complex; they combine
state services, political authorities and popular participation,
and all these down to the village level. But public funds
seep away at the middle level, the base gives more than it
receives, and foreign aid is still concentrated on urban
centres, the more-developed regions and large-scale
projects.

A major failure, given the stated objectives of health
policy, is the relative neglect of village health workers—the
focus of popular participation. Lachenmann explains this in
terms common in analyses from around the world:

the interaction of various mutually strengthening political, economic,
organisational and sociocultural factors. Both the people and state
employees in a district which has been exposed to a continuing process
of underdevelopment for many decades feel neglected, exploited and
unrepresented at central level [Lachenmann, 1982: 121].

One consequence of this continuing failure to develop the
rural areas is a reinforcement of the tendencies for the
modern élite to stay in the urban centres. Information of
conditions in remote areas remains scanty, the centralistic
tendencies of the state and the self-interest of the state
bureaucracy are strengthened. Complexity of practice and
scarce resources may result in resignation in those responsible for the implementation of policy—however progressive
that policy might be. Lachenmann concludes:

The inconsistency between the defence of modern privileges and the
adoption of the development patterns of industrialised countries on the
one hand and attempts to achieve self-sufficient, collective development
on the other will increase the tendency towards technocratic systems;
planning is done on a high level, making it impossible for the people to
assume responsibility and to participate [p. 122].

Smoking and Health
In 1979 the WHO Expert Committee on Smoking Control
described how the habit spread from country to country and
continent to continent. Consumption of tobacco is growing

fastest in the poorest countries of the world and 'smoking diseases will appear in developing countries before communicable diseases and malnutrition have been controlled and . . . the gap between the rich and poor countries will thus be further expanded' (World Health Organisation, 1979: 8). According to the Food and Agricultural Organisation, consumption of cigarettes will continue to rise at a much faster rate in the poor countries than in the rich; in 1976 two-thirds of United States tobacco shipments were to developing countries (Muller, 1978).

Wickström (1979), in a study of cigarette marketing, describes the increase in consumption in Ghana, Kenya, Malaysia and Thailand. In all four countries there was an annual per capita growth in consumption of 2 per cent; sales were far outstripping population growth. In Thailand, smoking was spreading rapidly to young people of 14 or 15 years old and to women. Between 1970 and 1977, cigarette sales by the Thai Tobacco Monopoly increased by more than 50 per cent. The 'growth segments' of the market in Ghana are among men between 18 and 35 years of age; it is estimated that between 35 and 40 per cent of Ghanain men smoke.

In both Kenya and Malaysia smoking was seen as a sign of sophistication and modernism, and increases dramatically with the level of education and income. The fastest growth is again among the young male population.

Not surprisingly, there is increasing evidence from developing countries of tobacco-related morbidity and mortality (Population Information Program, 1979; Roemer, 1982).

In very many countries, the transnational tobacco conglomerates are active in encouraging the growing of tobacco as a cash crop: 'they deliver a package—advice, finance and markets. Other crops, without the same efficient system, cannot compete' (Muller, 1978: 58).

Not only are the poor countries consuming more tobacco, and increasingly producing themselves for the transnational conglomerates, but the tar and nicotine contents of the cigarettes marketed there appear to be very much higher. This was referred to as 'the double standard of the tobacco companies selling one type of cigarette domestically and another type of the same brand but with higher levels of toxic constituents elsewhere', by a meeting of UN agencies in 1981 (Roemer, 1982: 89).

It is also widely reported that there is an absence of effective legislation controlling advertising, and that 'tobacco manufacturers have no hesitation in subjecting developing countries to many of the most cynical and discredited forms of advertising that are no longer acceptable in most western countries' (Gray and Daube, 1980: 98).

Smoking is universally a problem for social policy. In the poor countries it is in most areas a relatively new phenomenon, associated with 'modernisation' and constituting a very serious threat to present and future health. There can surely be little doubt that growing tobacco in countries with serious malnutrition demonstrates the profound problems faced by social policy. How can poor countries control the smoking epidemic? Phasing out tobacco production would help, but is extremely difficult in face of demands for cash-crop income. It is also a long-term change demanding co-operation across many agencies. The dynamics of an externally oriented economy will determine the pattern of economic activity; tobacco is but a particularly clear example of this.

Health education is clearly important. But smoking competes with many other issues for attention. More important, the muted health message is far outweighed by the direct power of tobacco advertising and even more by the indirect power of public attitudes. The association of cigarette smoking with a high prestige, 'modern' life-style is the greatest obstacle to social policies directed at the problem of smoking and health.

A strategy which has gained widespread support is the enactment of comprehensive effective anti-smoking legislation. 'Legislation, in short, is the cornerstone for a comprehensive programme of smoking control' (Roemer, 1982: 90). But how realistic is this in the context of poor countries? Anxious for more cash-crop production, more manufacturing and revenue for taxes, the great majority of governments give anti-smoking legislation very low priority. Moreover, public opinion backed by very powerful economic interests is generally opposed. In this, smoking stands for a number of other issues; alcohol, pharmaceuticals, baby-milk, 'Western' food, are further examples (World Health Organisation, 1980; 1981c; 1982b). The effects on health are known; these are crucial issues for social policy, but they are not essentially health issues. The problem is primarily an ideological and political one, legislative and administrative practice, developed over a very long period, to support the commercial objective, are ill-suited to the kind of control necessary to fight the smoking epidemic.

Some countries have attempted to implement policies in this area; the Arab states are notable in the extent and strength of measures taken in the past five years (Roemer, 1982: 93–4). But a World Health Organisation survey of legislation showed that in 1982 only a tiny number of poor countries had enacted anti-smoking laws. In Africa, only Mozambique had a ban on advertising and was also the only country with mandatory health education. No Latin American state had a total ban on advertising, although a number had partial controls and required 'health warnings' on packaging. In South-East Asia, India, Sri Lanka and Thailand had similar controls. The only other state reported to have a total ban on advertising and a number of other controls was Singapore; Malaysia also, in the Western Pacific region, had some controls (Roemer, 1982: 107–12).

A great deal remains to be done if the rapid spread of smoking and its destruction of health is to be controlled. The dilemmas faced by social policy in the poor countries are cruel in the extreme.

Oral Rehydration Therapy
As outlined earlier, the greatest killer of small children in the world is diarrhoea. One child in the poor world dies from this cause every six seconds. Diarrhoea kills through dehydration; it is almost always the loss of water and salt that brings about death. The body will fight off pathogens in a few days—there are in any case no known drug treatments for most diarrhoeal pathogens. Therapy need only

replace lost salt and fluid. Oral rehydration is cheap and effective:

The recipe for oral rehydration salts is very simple: the critical ingredients are 20 grams of glucose and 3.5 grams of salt to a litre of water . . . sugar will do, at 40 grams to the litre. UNICEF's packets of salts . . . are a little more sophisticated: they include 2.5 grams of sodium bicarbonate (baking soda) and 1.5 grams of potassium chloride, both elements that are lost in the diarrhoeal stool. While neither of these is essential to the treatment, they improve its effectiveness. Fortunately, potassium is found in many tropical fruits, including bananas, papaya and green coconut water [Rohde, 1983: 72].

Oral rehydration therapy is of enormous significance for health in the poor countries. Many millions of lives can be saved, and the suffering of many millions more dramatically reduced. In a number of studies the use of oral rehydration salts (ORS) for treating dehydrated children at the community level has decreased the number of deaths from diarrhoea by as much as between 50 and 60 per cent over a one-year period (World Health Organisation, 1983b).

Of massive importance to health policies and programmes, the treatment is *simple*. It can be given by health workers with only minimal training but, more important, can be given early by parents themselves. The use of ORS involves people directly in the care of their children and gives health workers opportunities to communicate vital health education messages on diarrhoea prevention and nutrition. In all important respects this is one of the greatest health advances for many decades. It is made supremely important by its accessibility to ordinary people. Giving people knowledge, and the power to act on that knowledge is the key not only to successful health education programmes but to the primary health care approach itself (World Health Organisation, 1983c). Oral rehydration is a crucial part of primary health care; it is an effective treatment for 90 per cent of cases of acute diarrhoea. To protect children from diarrhoeal infection requires action on many fronts—health and nutrition education, more clean water and safer sanitation, improved hygiene and immunisation against diarrhoea-inducing infections like measles are but the major ones. But dehydration kills, and rehydration can save many lives. UNICEF's *State of the World's Children 1984* documented some successes (UNICEF, 1983: 37–9):

- In Guatemala, child deaths halved in an area with a population of 64,000 after 'health promoters' began teaching mothers how to use locally made packets of oral rehydration salts.
- In Costa Rica, child deaths from dehydration dropped by more than 80 per cent in hospitals since ORT was introduced.
- In Honduras, diarrhoea deaths among children under the age of 2 halved by the use of ORT. After one year of a health education campaign 95 per cent of mothers knew how to make and administer the salts.
- In Bangladesh, 900 field-workers have taught 2.5 million women how to make ORT solutions from salt and molasses. More than 90 per cent of mothers can now prepare an effective mix and many are now using it.
- In Nicaragua, 80,000 young literacy workers spread knowledge of ORT. From being the leading cause of child death in 1980, diarrhoeal infection had dropped to fifth place by 1982.

There continue to be technological advances in oral rehydration; the use of cereal-based solutions, for example. But fundamental issues remain, and they are social policy issues. To achieve maximum effectiveness from ORT demands a reorientation of health systems, the active involvement of communities and a rejection of much conventional wisdom, not least deeply entrenched attitudes to medical interventions and drug treatments.

just as glucose and salt are the two vital ingredients of the 'technological breakthrough', so support of the national community through all available means of communication and the use of new kinds of local community development workers are the two vital ingredients in the 'social breakthrough' which is as necessary as the salts themselves if ORT is to play its part in a child health revolution [UNICEF, 1983: 41].

Social Policy, Health and Development
This brief outline of only a few aspects of the health issues facing social policy in the poor countries has illustrated several themes introduced earlier. The significance of outside influence in welfare institutions, attitudes and policies is clear. So too are the constraints imposed by economic and social formations. New approaches have emerged, often

in the most difficult conditions; these new approaches share
a concern with basic needs and a search for low-cost effective solutions to major problems. Above all, successful policies share a drive towards the reorientation of welfare
institutions—away from the overwhelming domination of
professionals in a repressive hierarchy and towards more and
more control by communities themselves. Health and development is marked by contradictions, cruel dilemmas and the
awful consequences of adverse change; but it also shows the
possibilities for organised action for welfare in a huge number
of ways across the whole spectrum of social contexts.

SOCIAL SERVICES FOR CHILD CARE

Nowhere are indecision and ineptitude so revealing as in the administration of laws relating to children wherein the failure to evolve a national
policy and a suitable administrative machinery for implementation reflects
the deplorable limits of societal apathy [Rao, 1979: 93].

Child-care services are dominated by legislation, and in most
of the world, although there is a law which in principle
safeguards the welfare of children, the rights and needs of
children are neglected in practice (MacPherson, 1984,
1987a). Part of that neglect is the consequence of the nature
of legislative and administrative forms. Part also is due to
the inappropriate welfare institutions existing in very many
states. The continuance of irrelevant policies and
programmes in many countries is to a considerable extent
a function of pre-existing laws and institutions. The impera-
tive of existing provision is extremely powerful. In this
section, a brief review of child-care legislation will be
followed by a short study of child-care services in India, as
an illustration of problems and policies in this field.
Discussion of successful approaches to child care will focus
on policies and services most clearly related to the needs of
the majority, in the context of development.

Child-Care Legislation
In very many states, existing legislation continues to reflect
extensive colonial influence. This is widely seen to be the

source of immense difficulty for the development of contemporary policies of programmes. Tara Ali Baig, President of the International Union for Child Welfare commented on this in relation to his own country:

in the welfare field, the imitation of Western legal systems and training of professional workers introduced systems into India that were ill-adapted to India's needs. The focus of both stemmed from industrial societies such as Britain and America . . . Laws were consequently instituted in India with a correctional bias instead of a development bias, and even today the West Bengal Children's Act brackets delinquents and destitutes who continue to be housed together in prisons or prison-like institutions established under the law. [Baig, 1979: 4].

The most comprehensive review of child welfare legislation in recent years (Pappas, 1983) shows clearly how the inappropriateness of existing legislation affects states in all parts of the world. Current efforts to improve child welfare legislation are marked by two general themes: first, the desire to replace inappropriate colonial law with indigenous law; second, the wish to retain important elements of traditional or customary laws, either within the newly created legislation or as a complementary system. In child welfare this is a particularly significant feature of contemporary developments as it is traditional law which embodies the patterns of responsibility for the care and protection of children.

These two major trends produce considerable tension in many legal systems and provide a vivid illustration of the struggle between competing pressures and influences in welfare and social policy. In Cameroon, for example, child offenders face a legal system which has three legislative traditions, as the present state is a fusion of a French and a British colony (Djeudjang, 1977). Similar difficulties are reported from the Congo (Tchibinda and Mayetela, 1983), where the laws governing care of orphans, adoption, foster care and guardianship are found in the Civil Code of 1904, which was based on the Napoleonic Code. These inherited laws co-exist uneasily with other laws relating to child welfare enacted since independence. In other legal systems, with very different legal forms, the same essential problems are found. The Philippines has the burden of laws derived from periods of rule under different colonial powers (Romero, 1979). In Latin America, a number of states have complex patterns of law reflecting Spanish, Portugese and other European influences, as well as more recent influences from, for example, the United States. De Duran (1983), discussing child welfare legislation in Colombia, sees this as a major obstacle to the development of relevant and effective law in this field. In a few cases, extensive legislative reform has been undertaken in an effort to facilitate and encourage social change of a particular kind. Cuba provides a dramatic example of this in relation to child welfare law (Azicri, 1980; Finlay, 1983).

Most states however continue to grapple with the problems of legislative systems whose roots and guiding principles are frequently alien in crucial respects. The dilemmas in the search for appropriate child welfare law in the context of rapid social change are very real; Rwezaura identified this in the Tanzanian case:

due to the weakened traditional forms of social control, the courts seem to offer an authoritative forum in which issues involving the control of children are to be resolved. Unfortunately . . . courts are not prepared to help. In this continuing tug-of-war between the state and the peasant family, the status of the child continues to remain in great doubt [Rwezaura, 1977: 93].

Social Services
Social services in general have low priority in poor countries and are still dominated by essentially remedial approaches. In the majority of states, organised social services for children are minimal and frequently bear little relation to the child welfare needs and priorities. Non-government organisations are particularly active in this aspect of social service activity, and there are very many states in which the entire field of, for example, residential child-care provision is the responsibility of voluntary and charitable organisations, many of them having a history of such activity which began in the colonial period (Chaturvedi, 1979; MacPherson, 1982; Caplan, 1985). In virtually all countries services have been urban-centred and have been overwhelmingly based on

imported Western approaches and forms (Rodriguez, 1976; Acosta, 1976; Midgley, 1981; Onokerhoraye, 1984).

Thus most poor countries have inherited, and continue to operate, child welfare services which are primarily concerned with the provision of residential care, responses to child offenders, and the management of legal provisions for adoption and foster care. Although the need for all of these is widely acknowledged, it is the inappropriateness of such concerns as the central themes of child welfare policies which dominates the contemporary debate.

This was very clearly reflected in the documents produced during and as a consequence of the 'International Year of the Child' in 1979. Considerable emphasis was put on poverty and inequality as fundamental causes of the problems threatening children, and two themes were clearly visible in the policies being advocated—an emphasis on basic needs and the encouragement of community-based services (UNICEF, 1982). The pursuit of development-oriented services in rural areas as opposed to remedial services, largely in towns, is characteristic of initiatives associated with community-based programmes (UNICEF, 1985). In recent years increasing emphasis has been put on mobilising communities to free themselves from dependency on 'traditional' social services and begin a process of self-development. There have been very many outstanding successes in countries around the world—many examples of imaginative and innovative programmes which have given communities new strength and given children an infinitely better life (MacPherson, 1987a). But the realities of poverty and underdevelopment are such as to place very severe limitations on what people can do for themselves. Beyond those limitations there are enormous obstacles placed by organised welfare systems, expressed in law and operated by professionals not infrequently dedicated to the policies and approaches which have for so long held sway (Midgley, 1981).

Services for Children in India

The Indian example illustrates many aspects of the child welfare problem. India itself is a vast country; it contains a sixth of all the world's children and within its borders encompasses a great range of social, religious and cultural forms (Chaturvedi, 1979; Gokhale and Sohoni, 1979). There is a complex legal system, very heavily influenced by a long period of colonial rule, with a proliferation of state laws. A number of commentators have identified the law as a major barrier in the development of child welfare legislation (Gokhale, 1975; Gangrade, 1978; Jain and Loghani, 1979).

Organised child-care services in India have been dominated by many thousands of non-government organisations, with an emphasis on institutional care, primarily in urban areas (India, 1974; Bedi, 1978; UNICEF, 1978). There has been considerable growth in the use of foster care as an alternative to residential care, but this is hampered by a lack of staff and resources for adequate supervision (Lalitha, 1977). There are, in addition, very considerable cultural and social problems with the use of foster care. Alternative forms have been developed in some areas; for example, the SOS children's villages, which aim to provide an environment closer to that of ordinary family life. This programme is funded entirely by sponsorships (Baig, 1979). There are very many efforts to establish care facilities which are very different from the institutions of the past.

But absolute increases in the amount of child-care provision, or changes in the law, do not benefit the majority of children in need. There are estimated to be nearly 2 million orphaned children in India, and facilities for only a very tiny fraction of that number. Rao comments that 'With nearly a hundred million children living below the poverty line, the élite discussions as to who is a neglected child lose all meaning, because exploitation, exposure and abandonment are the direct consequences of degrading poverty' (Rao, 1979: 97).

The Children Acts govern both children in need of care and young offenders (Jacob, 1979; Jain, 1979). The legislation demands an elaborate administrative system and complex institutional machinery, following models developed in affluent societies. The juvenile justice system demonstrates this with particular force. The law requires that the juvenile offenders be kept in a 'place of safety', that reports are written on them and their families by probation officers, and that they be dealt with by specially constituted juvenile courts assisted by honorary social workers. There is a great deal that is good in the formal system of juvenile justice in India, and in very many respects the provisions are in advance of many other countries. But the elaborate and costly system for administering juvenile justice bears no relation to the needs of children. In 1977 the Children Acts covered only 197 of the 370 districts in the country. There were 80 juvenile courts and about 150 observation homes. The number of children's homes was around 90 and there were 85 certified schools and analogous institutions for delinquent children. The total capacity of all these institutions was about 15,000 while every year about 150,000 children are apprehended by the police (Rao, 1979: 98).

Despite enormous achievements, particularly in the past ten years, the provision of child-care services in India has not been able to address more than a fraction of the problem. There are shortages of money and staff, difficulties of planning and administration. But above all, Indian critics of child-care services point to the inappropriateness of these forms of provision in a country which is 80 per cent rural and poor. The burden of inherited legislation, imported concepts and outside influence are seen to be very great.

A contrasting example may be found in the provision of day-care facilities, where India has developed innovative policies and programmes, in both urban and rural areas.

The mobile crèches programmes in Delhi and Bombay is a response to the needs of the young children who accompany their mothers to work on large construction sites. They camp with their parents and move from one site to another. In 1969 one woman began a movement by setting up a tent on one work-site in Delhi (Bridgland, 1972; Mahadevan, 1977). In 1970, Mobile Crèches was registered as an independent voluntary organisation. By 1974 it began working with children of the poorest working mothers in resettlement colonies; in 1979 there were 101 centres in Delhi and 47 in Bombay (Singh, 1979). At that date there were 244 full-time and 19 part-time staff, all of whom were local and all paid. The programme has a number of aims beyond the provision of day-care facilities itself, although this remains the key feature of the work. Essentially, the provision of basic child-care facilities is used as the focus for a range of activities, including literacy, health, nutrition, education, community organisation, publicity. Singh's description of the problems facing children in these areas underlines themes discussed earlier:

There is a severe erosion in health of the younger children (0–5 years) due to the poor facilities and the neglect caused by the mother's lack of time. The older children are tied up with survival chores cooking, collecting/stealing firewood, supplementing income by selling berries, etc., and in providing physical safety for younger children and their meagre possessions. The worksite offers them hardly any other learning experiences and migrancy denies them the chance of schooling. They live in a harshly commercial situation and are cut off from the sources of emotional sustenance and knowledge which their parents derived from a traditional agricultural way of life. They are therefore growing up psychologically and physically less equipped for the fight for marginal existence [Singh, 1979: 360–1].

Again, relative to the level of need, the mobile crèche programme is tiny. But it serves as an example of thousands of programmes of this kind, which are essentially responses to need, evolving methods over a period of time and with a philosophy of action and participation. Mobile Crèches, in common with very many other successful child welfare programmes relies on discussion, feedback and local-level planning in response to specific problems.

In much broader terms, similar themes can be seen in the programme of rural child-care centres and in the national policy of integrated child-development services (India, 1975; Khandekar, 1979; Venkataswamy and Kabir, 1979). In keeping with the priority of problems facing children in rural India, there is a heavy emphasis on health and nutrition, but very many other activities have become associated with these programmes. The need for policies which respond to basic needs, in ways which are feasible, manageable and allow for the education and involvement of local communities is consistently demonstrated in surveys of these and other aspects of child welfare in India.

Social Security
In the developing countries, social security provision and
the legislation governing it shows the domination of outside
influence more directly and explicitly than perhaps any other
area of social welfare (Midgley, 1984a; MacPherson, 1987b).
In virtually every country forms of social security have been
modelled on those in the industrialised countries (Malloy,
1979; Musiga, 1980; Johri and Schri, 1982). In many cases
the legal provisions were little changed, and frequently not
at all; in recent years a number of states have been
attempting to reform their social security laws in an effort to
make them more appropriate (ILO, 1982; Midgley, 1984a:
105–15).

There are several common characteristics in countries
around the world. First, restriction to those in formal wage
employment. In many countries, indeed, it is only relatively
recently that coverage has been extended to even most of
those in full-time wage employment (Mallet, 1980; Elogo,
1980; Montas, 1983; Gruat, 1984). In very many states cover
remains restricted to those in the most highly paid and
secure employment. The link between formal wage employment and participation in social security schemes is virtually
universal, whether the specific form of provision is based
on provident funds or social insurance. The obvious effect
of this link is that schemes cover only a very tiny proportion
of populations; in India, for example, only some 5 million
workers are covered in a country with a population over 600
million (Johri and Schri, 1982). Among the small minorities
which are covered, there is extreme bias in the quality of
provision, in favour of the more highly paid and toward
men. Even the most fully developed social security systems
in Third World countries channel resources to a very small
and relatively very privileged section of the national
community. Indeed, it may plausibly be argued that the
more sophisticated and extensive a social security system is,
if it is built on 'social insurance' principles the more unfair
and inequitable it will be. Resources may in fact be chan-
nelled from the poorer sections of the community to the
better-off through the mechanisms of social security funding
and resource distribution (Mesa-Lago, 1983). Given the

economic conditions in developing countries, any substantial extension of social insurance protection is extremely difficult; coverage of whole populations is impossible. There are constant improvements to existing schemes, but these most often represent a widening of inequalities and a further division between privileged minorities and disadvantaged majorities.

Poor countries face a cruel dilemma; the benefits under existing schemes may be meagre and inappropriate, coverage very limited and need intense—the pressures for urgent improvement are real and powerful. On the other hand, the needs of the great mass of people demand attention. If social security systems are to meet any part of those needs, they have to shift their focus and adopt new approaches which do not allow for improvement in conventional terms. Existing provision most often owes its origin, its continuation and its growth to outside influences and the replication, within poor countries, of approaches in the industrialised countries. Minority groups within poor countries place very high demands on such provision and pressure strongly and effectively for their extension.

These realities make the pursuit of genuine social security extremely difficult; countries which are concerned with the welfare of the majority must examine the overall effects of existing and proposed social security provision on resource distributions throughout society. As noted earlier, social security systems are rarely, if ever, neutral in their distributional impact; they seem in virtually all cases to be effecting net transfers in favour of the better-off. Mesa-Lago (1983) has identified a variety of factors contributing to this 'regressive transference' within conventional social security schemes. Even where the regressive impact is minimised, the social security organised on the basis of rights established through formal wage employment will do nothing for the poor majority, who have at most only a marginal place in the formal wage economy. The vast majority in poor countries are still outside that economy. Thus, whatever is done to improve conventional social security, both to extend its scope and to make its provisions more relevant and appropriate, the major issue for social security remains: what can be done, through organised welfare institutions to provide some social security for those millions in desperate need?

Midgley, in a comprehensive review of social security and welfare in the third world, put considerable emphasis on the potential of social assistance (1984a). A brief examination of this form of social security will illustrate some possibilities for social security policies and programmes which are relevant to the needs of the poor majority.

In 1942 the International Labour Office defined social assistance as 'a service or scheme which provides benefits to persons of small means as of right in amounts sufficient to meet minimum standards of need, and financed from taxation' (ILO, 1942). This definition serves as well today, for any country, as it did more than forty years ago. The four elements are all crucial: restriction of benefits to those in need, adequate minimum benefits as a goal, benefits as of right, and funding from general taxation. Thus a social assistance approach can embody the notion that everyone should have 'rights to assistance', in the same way that they have a 'right to health'. The enormous problems of implementing those rights in the short or even the medium term should not obscure their fundamental importance.

In terms of the distributional aspects of social security, the nature of funding is clearly crucial; the nature of the taxation system will be reflected in any social assistance scheme. Only if taxation is progressive may social assistance be part of a substantial redistribution between income groups (Montas, 1983). In social assistance, there is an approach which seems to hold the potential to meet some of the needs of the poor in developing countries where existing schemes do not. Social assistance might be adopted more widely as an approach and the principles used in the formation of programmes designed to have maximum impact. There are a number of examples of the innovative use of social assistance in different parts of the world (Midgley, 1984a, 1984c; MacPherson, 1986b). There are severe limitations on all forms of social welfare in poor countries, but progress is possible and innovations are possible. Around the world there are attempts to work out original solutions which do not copy existing Western models, despite the perpetuation of destructive attitudes and approaches—above all, the pervasive influence of poor-law values and beliefs (Midgley, 1984c). Some examples will illustrate these attempts.

The Indian state of Kerala has provided a powerful example of approaches to genuine primary health care, and it is perhaps significant that social security provision in Kerala has similarly been developed in ways which make it more relevant to the needs of the poorest. The major schemes, which took effect in the late 1970s and early 1980s, are pensions for agricultural workers, pensions and allowances for the destitute, unemployment allowances, and a series of schemes relevant to those who are self-employed in the agricultural sector. Among the latter, crop and cattle insurance schemes, organised for the poorest farmers, may be seen to be of much more practical relevance than any other form of provision for groups who depend entirely or mainly on their crops or cattle and for whom crop failure or sickness or death of cattle is a disaster.

Provision of benefits for the unemployed are means-tested and subject to strict regulation; for example, unemployment assistance is only paid after three years of registered unemployment, and there are conditions attached to its payment:

The beneficiaries are under obligation to help the State in promoting adult education and implementing small-scale irrigation schemes; they should participate in rural development schemes and help in promoting the sanitation and cleanliness drive initiated by local administration and help in housing schemes [Nair, 1980: 72].

In addition, Kerala has an 'employment generation scheme' under which the unemployed also participate in rural development schemes. This use of social assistance as part of a programme of employment creation has been noted elsewhere. Particularly in relation to the so-called 'informal sector', a number of countries have schemes which provide small loans to enable the establishment of small businesses. Midgley describes the Self-Employment Assistance Programme in the Philippines which, he suggests, 'is now regarded by the Government as a preferable method of providing help assistance to needy families and is widely used' (Midgley, 1984a: 259). That particular scheme is operated by the Philippines Ministry of Social Welfare, and although severely limited in the number of people helped (147,000 individuals in 1980), it is reported that the average incomes of beneficiaries had increased by approximately 98 per cent, and only a small minority had defaulted on their loans (Reidy, 1980). There are clearly very many difficulties in using social assistance in this way, and the approach will only be relevant to a relatively small proportion of the population. But this is an example of creative use of social assistance which could be implemented much more widely, in a variety of forms.

The number of old people without resources of their own, or the support of relatives, is growing rapidly; in terms of social security cover, only an extremely small number have any sort of pension. Social assistance is used in many countries to relieve the most abject poverty and destitution of the old, but in general this provision is extremely meagre, subject to great local variation and often administered with extremely harsh conditions, including the use of residential institutions into which the poor must go if they are to receive any relief (ISSA, 1982).

The Secretary-General of the International Social Security Association wrote in 1982 that:

In the developing countries, the problems raised by the need for social protection of older persons are even more complex: whilst the aim of bringing resources and needs closer together is clear, the ways in which this can be achieved are not. Certainly the developing countries need to be encouraged to seek new ways of achieving suitable forms of social protection, which should include efforts to safe-guard better than have the industrialised countries the traditions of family solidarity and mutual aid which are still very much alive there [Rys, 1982: 488].

As with unemployment Kerala provides an interesting example; in addition to pension provision for the minority in formal wage employment, there are schemes for groups generally excluded by social security. From 1980 agricultural workers over 60 were entitled to a monthly pension of 45 rupees. But they must have been resident in Kerala for not less than five years and have an annual income of less than 1,500 rupees. Provision in Kerala is clearly more extensive and more generous than in many other states in India—the average social assistance payment to the elderly being about half of the payment in Kerala.

These examples of the use of social assistance in practice indicate that if social security is to make any significant contribution to fighting poverty in developing countries, it must change its nature. As with health, the emphasis must be on the production of relevant programmes, locally administered and controlled, financed from progressive national taxation and embodying rights to benefits.

In a survey of social security provision in Latin America, Mesa-Lago pointed to perhaps the single most difficult aspect of this transformation:

the elimination of some benefits and the reduction of excessively generous conditions enjoyed by the most privileged groups . . . it is not financially possible to have both universal coverage and massification of privilege . . . However, the implementation of reform would have to overcome strong economic and political obstacles [Mesa-Lago, 1983: 104, 106].

He concludes that 'the greatest potential for change lies among those unprotected; they should be educated and organised to demand a more equitable system of social security that fulfils its principles and essential objectives' (p. 108).

Johri and Schri, in an examination of the prospects for social security in India, make the same case:

It is probable that until the poor and the weak are able to get organised and acquire political muscle, they cannot be sure that the slender allocations the Government is prepared to make will necessarily reach them. On the other hand, even if the delivery systems are improved, they would continue to rest on the principle of welfare and government handouts, quite incompatible with the concept of social security-based contributions, rights and claims on the one hand, and shared social convictions supported by a competent administration on the other [Johri and Schri, 1982: 106].

It is clearly right to stress the need for organisations of the poor; there is no doubt that redistributive social security is a political issue. Furthermore, grassroots organisations

could provide the basis for locally administered, decent-
ralised, innovative and relevant social security administration. It is equally right to attack social security provision
which is in the form of 'handouts'; there must be *rights* to
benefits.

As with primary health care, there is enormous potential
for original solutions to social security problems. In relation
to social assistance, and to social welfare services in general,
there are some hopeful signs, despite conditions which are
extremely hostile and the existence of policies which are
irrelevant or worse. But, as Ignacy Sachs believes:

the richness and diversity of community traditions give us reason to hope
that Third World societies will be able to learn from our mistakes and
will embark resolutely on the path of the self-production of social services,
with the encouragement of active support of the State—in a word, that
they will bypass the historical stage of the Welfare State. In this way
they may find new and original expressions, rooted in their cultures and
institutions, of the universal values enshrined in the right to development
[Ignacy Sachs 1982: 144].

6 Relevance for Social Policy in the North

We have tried in the preceding chapters to indicate something of the realities of social issues in the poor countries of the world. We have also suggested a number of common themes in social policy responses to those issues. Our concern throughout has been to engage all those concerned with social welfare in a consideration of problems and responses in often unfamiliar contexts. Earlier chapters have elaborated on this and laid out some of the ways in which we feel such consideration to be vital.

In this chapter we seek to outline some specific linkages between contemporary social welfare in poor countries to that in rich countries. As we have argued elsewhere, these terms are in themselves inadequate and perhaps misleading; we are seeking to establish the case for a 'global perspective'. Before attempting to do that by examining some particular issues, let us briefly summarise our major themes.

Poverty dominates the lives of the vast majority of the world's people. There is now a far greater common awareness of the magnitude and urgency of their needs than ever before. But equally there is widespread doubt as to whether the approaches to development which have prevailed for many years will bring an end to misery and deprivation. In terms of social policy, the dilemmas of continuing underdevelopment have forced a radical examination of planned social change and particularly of the role of organised welfare, in all its forms.

In broad outline, we have seen that in terms of welfare, 'development' efforts have too often failed the mass of ordinary people. Development plans are still primarily based on a 'trickle-down' theory of economic and social development. Large-scale projects are initiated and controlled from the top, building up a national infrastructure of industry and services, with the hope that eventually all citizens will benefit from them as their effects move downwards through the society. From the perspective of human welfare this has not often produced the desired results. Changes beneficial to the quality of life have not, in fact, 'trickled-down' to the poor. Many of them are no better-off than before, some may be considerably worse-off. Despite the undoubted progress which has been made, some of which can be measured, the balance sheet shows a very heavy burden on the poorest.

Furthermore, many attempts by poor countries to provide essential services, and to direct social change towards an enhanced quality of life for the mass of people, have been perverted. Most commonly, services have been based on sophisticated and expensive models from the industrialised world. These have been shown to be inappropriate in many different contexts but exhibit powerful tendencies for survival, expansion and reproduction. Such approaches consume huge proportions of available resources, making impossible the extension of services beyond a small part of the population.

The inequalities of condition in most of the world are matched by gross inequalities in social welfare response. Across the range of issues we have touched on, the inadequacy of conventional social policies to significantly benefit the lives of the great majority has been clear. Again and again, the need for entirely new approaches has been seen—approaches which focus directly on people themselves and which are suited to their particular conditions, resources and aspirations. Such approaches must not only recognise the economic, social and political forces ranged against the interests of the poor majority but must also acknowledge the extent of human diversity. These approaches must embody the essential purpose of social welfare—the welfare of individuals in their communities. The enormity of the issues may induce paralysis of thought, despair or a sense of hopelessness. These are luxuries the people of the poor countries cannot afford. If nothing else, the evidence of the achievement of social welfare in the worst conditions gives those of us who can afford those luxuries some cause for thought. This chapter is a deliberate attempt to suggest the relevance of 'welfare and development' to social welfare and social policy in the rich countries of the world. It is partial, at times oversimplified and possibly overstated. It is hoped that if interest is aroused, the topics will be pursued.

If there is one trend which has major contemporary importance in the social policy of poor countries, it is that towards 'basic services'. Put simply, these are services at the community level in maternal and child health, safe-water supply, food production and nutrition, literacy and elementary education, accessible housing, meaningful employment, and measures to improve the position of women.

Over the past decade such services and programmes have gained ground in very many countries, together with concerted efforts to shift the directions of social policy to the needs of majority populations. The key element in the 'basic services' approach—indeed in all attempts to build relevant social welfare programmes—has been emphasis on the active participation of the people themselves in projects and services from which they and their communities will benefit. In a number of fields this has been achieved to a remarkable extent, such that real development is not just stimulated from the top but also by building structures from the bottom upwards. In hundreds of thousands of communities the interest and creative energies of the people have been mobilised. But mobilisation is about power, and in very many cases the forces of the wider context in which communities must function have crushed attempts to improve the most basic conditions of life. Attempts to ensure provision for essential needs in these ways have been neither a panacea nor a disaster. They must, on balance, be seen as a profoundly important part of a dramatic shift in conceptions of social welfare policy. The implications of such approaches for overall patterns of policy, planning and resource distribution have sharpened awareness of fundamental issues and focused attention on the need for the establishment and maintenance of systems in which the interests of poor communities can be genuinely represented. In so doing, they inevitably raise questions regarding the control of social welfare, including that by professional groups.

Issues of resource distribution may be resolved in practice by the marginalisation of services for the poor. For example, 'self-help' basic services can be made to mean second-rate services provided by the poor themselves, from their own resources; the longer-run effects on better-off groups may be minimal. Similarly, the direct provision of low-cost 'relevant' services in poor communities may be used to justify the continuation of unequal and unjust resource distributions within service sectors. Basic services can alternatively be seen as a starting point from which more extensive and complete services will be added. The services themselves can often be seen as contributing to the development process itself. They are labour-intensive, they allow of some control by communities themselves, and they minimise the gulf between organised services and traditional social welfare systems. The improvements which can be achieved can often be gained rapidly, and these can more easily include significant changes for women and girls. In demonstrating the power of self-reliance, they may provide the basis for the development of other services and even open up the possibility of far-reaching community organisation. This is not to romanticise the approach; the immense practical problems are clear and the obstacles immense. Often the efforts of the many will be for the benefit of the few; most often the many will be women and the few will be men. But the power of the approach is real and has had an impact beyond what might have been imagined even twenty years ago.

For social policy, the support and encouragement of community-level services has become a major theme. The necessary reorientation of organisational structures, both government and non-government, has exposed the obstacles to welfare in many of those structures. Not least in the deployment of para-professional workers, engaged in activities which cut across boundaries hallowed by convention, the demands of these new approaches have very often been too much for systems to take. A common error is to seriously underestimate the deep conflicts of interests in poor countries, including those among 'the poor' themselves, and to assume aspirations and attitudes into existence, among those who should 'mobilise':

There can be no substitute for humility and realism in the élite consciousness that tries to serve the masses, and these qualities have been in short supply up to the present. The cause of participation has suffered from excessive manipulativeness, on the one hand, and from over-confidence in uniform mass readiness to participate on the other [Wolfe, 1981: 263].

The remainder of this chapter seeks to illustrate the illuminating power of contemporary trends in welfare and development. In part this is a conscious effort to contribute to the 'diffusion' of social policies and practices from the poor countries to the rich. To date, virtually all traffic has been in the opposite direction. As we have seen in earlier chapters, the growth of organised welfare in poor countries has been particularly affected by influences from the industrial countries. In short, and as Midgley (1984b) has argued elsewhere, a global perspective is needed to enhance social science understanding of social welfare and social policy.

A few examples are taken of issues in welfare, and a few aspects of those are examined in terms of the relevance of such a perspective. This cannot be more than illustrative; the treatment is partial, and the selection of issues is dictated by a wish to provide examples from a range of issues.

POVERTY

MacPherson (1983) has argued that, at least in Britain, the study of social welfare has almost entirely neglected the poor countries of the world. The study of poverty may be seen as a touchstone of the nature and extent of that neglect. It is surely beyond dispute that poverty, broadly defined, is the most fundamental concern of social policy in any society. It is at the heart of any conception of social welfare; discussions of its nature, its measurement, and responses to it, affect—directly and indirectly—virtually every aspect of social policy. Anyone concerned with welfare must face the complex and confusing issues which surround 'the concept of poverty' and the reality of the phenomenon in contemporary society. The greater part of the world is overwhelmingly dominated by poverty. The human experience in the world is one in which poverty takes a massive part in shaping the form and quality of that experience. Knowledge of poverty as a way of life is profound in most of the world, as too are the responses to the condition—spiritual, philosophical, social and practical. But virtually all discussion of poverty in industrial countries takes place with no reference to this vast wealth of experience, knowledge and perception. There has been virtually no development of a cross-national intellectual framework, despite the enormous amount of work done within different systems. There are very many reasons for this (MacPherson, 1983: 38–40), some of which may now be losing their former power. Certainly, outside the formal boundaries of academic study, concern with poverty is increasingly expressed in global terms, and the crucial linkages between economic and social systems are identified in explanations of that poverty. Three elements may be taken as illustrations; the need to set discussions of national poverty in an international context, the issues of 'poverty levels' and the nature of poverty as a lived experience.

As economic conditions in countries such as Britain continue to shift against vast numbers of poorer people, awareness of the global context in which the economy operates continues to grow. International finance and trade, together with associated political, military and professional formations set the parameters for national economies. Poverty in those economies must be seen in that same international context. Hundreds of millions of the world's people live in destitution; for a vast number of them, that destitution is a direct consequence of the actions of those economic institutions on which the 'prosperity' of the rich countries depend. The relationships between the peoples of the world are as crucial to poverty as they are to wealth. These relationships have for long been rooted in *underdevelopment*. Without an understanding of the realities of underdevelopment as a continuing process, responses to the continuing emiseration of much of the world will be flawed.

In 1986 UNICEF reports a worsening of the basic conditions of life in much of Africa, beyond the immediate and terrible issues of drought, famine and other disasters. The fundamental issues are identified as inappropriate approaches to development forced by continuing dependence within an international system operating for the benefit of the rich (UNICEF, 1986). Those concerned to understand poverty in the rich countries must also face the nature of international economic organisation. Through transnational corporations and international agencies such as the European Economic Community, the rich countries have not simply maintained their position but have in gross terms improved their relative position in the world. The cost for the poor within those rich countries has been great indeed. More and more, the actions of corporations in one part of the world directly affect workers in another. As production is shifted to 'low cost' economies and then to those with even lower cost, the consequences for individuals and communities can be devastating. Thus, any analysis of poverty within rich countries *must* be done within an international framework; explanations can only make sense if located in an understanding of the international forces acting on national economies.

The international context of poverty is also crucial to discussion of the second element: the definition and measurement of poverty. Subsistence poverty, relative poverty and social inequality are central to a continuous debate within the rich countries. As inequality increases, fuelled by economic and political change, this debate becomes more significant still. Wage rates are reduced, and more and more people are marginalised in relation to the formal economy. These trends are accompanied by erosion of the welfare provision which previously compensated, at least in part, for the unequal outcomes of economic competition. Social inequality has always been a fundamental theme in welfare and social policy. The poor countries have shown that economic growth does not lead to reduced inequality. In the context of international economic relationships, it can bring starkly polarised societies in which the wealthier classes co-exist with mass poverty. In very many countries there are coalitions of interest between those groups whose continued privileged existence depends on business and administration. This includes the salaried classes, most significantly those employed by the state, but also in some respects those few wage-earners who have achieved some measure of power. We have seen this in social security—it is painfully apparent also in health, housing, education and social services. Huge numbers of poor people have become not just relatively but absolutely worse-off as poverty and inequality increase. The continuing rise in the consumption of resources by privileged groups is a powerful theme in the social change observed. There are many who would now argue that these examples hold much for those industrial societies in which the gap between a massive group of poor and other groups widens remorselessly. Townsend argues that 'Social conditions in Britain are becoming polarised partly because of the internationalisation of manufacturing industry, finance, trade and defence. The analysis of poverty has to be placed in an international context' (Townsend, 1984: 35).

His analysis of poverty in contemporary Britain concludes that there is what can now justifiably be called 'mass' poverty, with 18 million poor people in a population of 60 million. But more, he identifies the hardening of class attitudes, as well as worsening economic conditions for the poor, as part of the explanation as to why 'areas of high unemployment in Britain are beginning to resemble in their squalor and social deprivation some of the worst features to be found in urban centres of poor countries' (p. 35). One response to greater numbers of poor people is to make worse the conditions for every one of them. In Britain we have seen this quite clearly, and current trends are all in the direction of a more divided welfare system. The definition of poverty itself is increasingly used both to disguise the extent of mass poverty and to minimise assistance to the poor. The current review of social security demonstrates above all a response to mass poverty; that response reduces rights to welfare, and lowers the living conditions of the poor.

The definition of poverty in rich countries is complex and elusive, but of profound importance. Ultimately it is in relation to that definition that welfare in general is conceived, and social policy shaped. It is about relative living conditions and participation in the life of the society in which people live. The poor countries most often contain both abject destitution and great wealth; but for most people within them the experience of significant social inequality is relatively new. The fundamental questions relating to any analysis of poverty demand a global perspective. Not least because, as Townsend suggests, 'The problem for most countries of the world is how social polarisation in the late twentieth century, with mass poverty and the social conflict and violence which mass poverty generates, may be avoided' (p. 34). But this leads into the third element; the *nature* of poverty itself. This is the most powerful yet the most elusive aspect of what might be drawn from study of welfare and society in poor countries. It is this which leads Seabrook to emphasise that 'It is the rich who threaten the stability of the world, not the poor' (Seabrook, 1984: 172). His '*Landscapes of Poverty*' sets images of contemporary poverty in Britain against those of the poorest urban people in India. The result is disturbing. Above all, it illustrates what underdevelopment *means*, both in the poor countries and the rich. The economic, social and political linkages are clear, and made starkly real in the lives of poor people.

Welfare demands consideration of essential values and elaboration of concepts rooted in those values. 'Poverty' is capable of shifting definition, with profound implications for policy and the poor. Within a perspective which is both historical and comparative, Seabrook challenges us to consider what lies at the roots of our contemporary Western version of poverty. Our wealth depends on the continued poverty of much of the world, and 'definitions of poverty in the rich world depend on ever-more convoluted and bizarre reformulations of what constitutes wealth' (Seabrook, 1984: 125). This focus on the nature of poverty is unsettling, certainly for conventional social welfare analysis. It is however, profoundly important. Seabrook uses the image of 'landscapes'; at the centre of his argument is the 'inner landscape' within each person, and in the rich countries this has been subject to massive demolition and reconstruction. It is an internal convulsion of human personality that is linked with the dominance of consumer markets. Why has this occurred? Because, in the rich countries, there was no longer scarcity—no one need be poor. But 'a sense of insufficiency, an experience of continuing privation could be maintained, even in the midst of an abundance unparalleled in human history' (Seabrook, 1984: 126).

This maintenance of need in conditions of plenty was seen by Tawney many years ago:

Mankind it seems, hates nothing so much as its own prosperity. Menaced with an accession of riches which would lighten its toil, it makes haste to redouble its labours, and to pour away the perilous stuff, which might deprive of plausibility the complaint that it is poor . . . the new resources . . . might have done something to exorcise the spectres of pestilence and famine . . . rulers, secular and ecclesiastical alike, thought otherwise. When pestilence and famine were ceasing to be necessities imposed by nature they re-established them by political art [Tawney, 1938: 85–6].

The 'political art' of the twentieth century is practised on a global scale; it has in our time brought 'the appropriation of human need'. This underpins the redefinition, in rich countries, or 'scarcity' itself and, it may be argued, the reformulation of poverty itself. Poverty, and illusions of scarcity, are essential power in the dynamic of systems in which 'enough' is anathema:

The maintenance of the subjective experience of being poor in the presence of its manifest redundancy has been at the heart of the transformation of the people; and it is to this end that the inner landscapes, the minds and feelings of women and men and children have been systematically reworked [Seabrook, 1984: 12].

The creation and recreation of new desires, new 'needs', inexhaustible and insatiable demands for 'products', is so pervasive it now eludes attention. But the significance of it, and the magic by which new and alien needs can be implanted, stand in direct comparison with the changes wrought in the patterns of life in poor countries. There, we see hundreds of millions engaged in agriculture to produce crops which fill no need for nutrition in the countries of their production. And for this the people have lost their means of subsistence. The tying of need to production and profit is indeed the most influential and most powerful part of what the rich countries have given to the world. Discussions of welfare must face the essential questions of the nature of needs. The equation of what we *buy*, or would seek to buy, with our *needs* raises the possibility that complex basic needs are untouched by material responses. If this is so, then there will be frustration and a restless search for more. It is this that, amid great wealth, 'has made sufficiency an impossible achievement' (Seabrook, 1984: 15).

This takes us to the very centre of the poverty question. Beyond minimal subsistence, poverty is felt experience; it is that which makes contemporary definitions within rich societies so difficult yet so important; for it is our concepts and definitions of poverty which are the starting point for so much of our construction and analysis of welfare. It is now conventional wisdom that concepts of poverty as *absolute* are inappropriate and misleading. The needs which people have are related to the society in which they live. That poverty is a relative not an absolute concept is now more or less accepted in the analysis of welfare (Townsend, 1979). Needs are therefore different in different societies; people are poor who are prevented by lack of resources from participating in the generally approved style of life in their society. But what if the creation and manipulation of need is itself a primary purpose of the society? What is poverty then? What are needs? This, argues Seabrook, is what has made definitions and remedies so difficult. Needs become measureless and so cannot be met:

This is what has defied judgements of what constitutes poverty in the West. It has made the well-to-do insecure, the affluent experience constant insufficiency, and even the very rich aware of their impoverishment. What we are dealing with is the expropriation of need . . . when . . . norms and standards are themselves all centred on fugitive notions of increase—more, better, higher, bigger, all of them comparative terms detached from their positive degree—then any definition of poverty becomes as mobile and untenable as any gesture towards sufficiency [Seabrook, 1984: 16].

Consideration of poverty in a global perspective forces awareness of the relationship between poverty and riches. But it forces also an awareness of the common ground between welfare in the poorest countries and welfare in the richest. Welfare is defined in terms of:

culture-specific norms, defined by people in specific societies, according to *their* criteria of what constitutes want or plenty, not standards deemed appropriate for them . . . Social want not asocial biological needs, define health and wealth [Worsley, 1984: 206].

Examining 'poverty', 'needs' and 'social wants' *across* societies sharpens our perception of 'impoverishment' as a concept, makes us more aware of what we have, and what we do not have. Impoverishment in rich countries is real, widespread, growing and demands attention. For any consideration of poverty, the creation, continuation and growth of impoverishment is central and must be understood in relation to goals of basic sufficiency. The global perspective forces consideration of the quality of life.

WOMEN AND WELFARE

A focus on the position of women has been one of the most dramatic and important shifts in the analysis of welfare in recent years (Morgan, 1984). Both for theory and practice, the power of analysis has grown alongside the organisation of women themselves. In this, there has been more of a coherent and conscious global perspective than in other aspects of the study of social welfare. But Roodkowsky, in a survey of the major writing on women and development, points out how recent the real growth of international exchange in ideas and information really is. She identifies 1975 as the 'turning point in the movement to bring a new relationship between women and development, by providing the impetus, the networks, the energy and the validity for a worldwide movement' (Roodkowsky, 1983: 14).

Since 1975 a great deal of perceptive and powerful material has been produced, much of it reflecting on

extremely important features of the women and development movement—a direct link with women themselves and
a bias towards development which comes from people.
Among the accounts of social change and women's perception of development, those recorded by Huston (1979) had
considerable impact. From conversations and interviews,
she reported the views of women on social and economic
change, health, education and politics. These were
accompanied by material from interviews with professionals
and 'leaders'. The result was a powerful testimony which
clearly illuminates the continuation of old oppressions and
the creation of new ones. But there was also growing awareness, determination and commitment to change.

A number of analysts have demonstrated the bias against
women in the majority of 'development' programmes.
Rogers (1980) pointed to the structural sexism of planning
agencies and their associated projects; she argued that
women must be integrated into projects as full and equal
participants in the planning process. While not disagreeing
with this, others have questioned the 'integration of women
into development' when that 'development' itself brings
patterns of economic and social change which serve to inten-
sify the exploitation of women, extend and entrench
inequalities, and destroy relationships.

Thus the work done by women, for women, questions the
nature of dominant approaches to development. In so
doing, many studies demonstrate how both men *and* women
are victims, although unequally. This emphasis on the
nature of the development process itself is crucial, but does
not detract from the need for analysis and action to confront
the structured inequality of women. It points to development efforts which are rooted in the power of communities
to define and direct the nature of change. In such efforts,
obstacles to the expression of women's power are very great;
women suffer both from their involvement in dependent
economics and their position in social systems:

Many of those writing about women's unequal position in society have
argued that if women had full access to the market . . . women's subordinate position in society would end. [We] reject such a view, arguing that

by concentrating solely on the process of production it ignores other fundamental causes of gender subordination. For the subordination of women continues when women enter the public sphere of wage labour, and also continues in societies where there has been a socialist transformation of the relations of production and distribution [Young *et al.*, 1980: *X*].

This dual oppression is fundamental to any policy response. As Palmer (1980) has argued, even a 'basic needs' approach will fail to serve the mass of women if the prior issue of women's power is not approached. Development strategies which emphasise the production of goods and services to meet the needs of the poorest may shift the burden for that production even further onto women without confronting the unequal social and political position of the mass of women. Palmer emphasises the mobilisation of women and with that mobilisation the need to specify and guarantee access to resources and rights to goods, both private and public. But even this will not be enough to meet women's needs. On many fronts, basic-needs programmes must be specifically biased to women if present inequalities are not to be carried forward. Thus many women now argue that in development, priorities must begin with the analysis of women's present position, proceed through specific programmes and be based on the mobilisation of women; that is, that development must be *for women* and not that women must work 'for development' as has most often been the case.

The relationship here between theory and practice is especially sharp. The relevance for specific policy areas is particularly clear, and in recent years community-based programmes, fuelled by incisive consciousness, have very often been initiated and developed by women, frequently in the face of powerful opposition. The force of change in just the past ten years has been very great. In general terms, the relevance of women's 'organisation for development' to welfare in the rich countries is clear, and clearly acknowledged. This was perhaps nowhere more visibly demonstrated than at the 1985 United Nations World Conference on Women, marking the end of the United Nations Decade for Women. Assessments of progress in the decade show that for the mass of women little has changed (United Nations, 1985). In most of the world women are in a worse position than before:

the modernisation and mechanisation of agriculture, the introduction of cash crops, training, credit and agricultural inputs continue, on the whole to be directed to men. For women, 'development' often means an increased workload, less access to land, and a decrease in their possibilities either to produce and market food and goods or to earn money . . . many policies and programmes have not only failed to improve their lives but have had detrimental effects upon them [Karl, 1984: 2].

Between 1975 and 1985, as economic conditions worsened so the consequences fell most heavily on women. But structural inequalities in political, social and cultural spheres continued, and in many areas worsened. Among the major obstacles to change which may be seen to operate in both rich and poor countries are:

the feminization of poverty on a global scale, continuing job segregation, wage disparities and disproportionate percentages of female unemployment, the increasing number of female-headed households (one-third of the world's homes) sex stereotyping . . . growing violence against women . . . At least now women have a common blueprint for change [Maloney, 1986: 56].

Thus most reports of the 1985 Conference stress those aspects of the decade which are seen to have produced the possibility of future action. In particular these relate, first, to massively increased awareness of the essential issues and, second, to the relationship between theory and practice in terms of the 'empowerment' of women. On the first of these, Anita Anand reports on responses to a questionnaire circulated before the conference to appraise the decade:

One particular response sums up the decade rather aptly: 'The results point, again and again, to the major underlying cause of women's inequality. A woman's domestic role as wife and mother—which is vital to the well being of the whole of society, and consumes around half her time and energy—is underpaid and undervalued [Anand, 1985: 14].

Another comment, from a participant in the very much larger NGO Forum, underlines the need for a global perspective:

the fact that the Forum spoke with many voices instead of one voice, is healthy and not negative. The exchange of information from all over the world on projects and programmes taking slightly different approaches to achieve broadly similar ends will have widened the horizons of women planning or implementing such activities. Just the sharing of experiences and perceptions will have served to increase women's feeling of being part of a world-wide movement with roughly comparative goals. In day-to-day work it is easy to lose sight of this [Nelson, 1986: 49].

In the area of women and welfare the theoretical work done in a global perspective is profound, and more explicitly linked with practice than in any other. The issues raised and the responses demanded are fundamental to the consideration of welfare in all societies.

A dramatic collection of essays published at the end of the decade reflects this very clearly. Debbie Taylor's Preface indicates vividly the power of the global perspective:

Discrimination against women is a profound and subtle sickness that has lodged itself deep in the subconscious of both men and women as well as in the structure of our societies . . . [but] today governments can no longer placidly assume that women are inferior. They must defend their position on a world stage [Taylor, 1985: 1].

In consideration of women and welfare, the work done within a global perspective is perhaps more extensive and more explicitly linked with practice than in any other. The issues raised and the responses demanded are fundamental to the consideration of welfare in all societies.

HEALTH

Analysis of *health* issues, when these are examined outside the constraints of 'medicine' or 'health services', demands the same wide-ranging recourse to social theory as we have seen in relation to other issues. Both in rich and poor countries health issues are increasingly seen in social, economic and political terms. But in the poor countries, illness and premature death are more extensive, and more devastating. Resources are desperately short and the lists of health problems almost infinitely long. The emergence of 'primary health care' as we saw earlier, was only partly a product of theoretical analysis; on the ground it was most often the product of absolute necessity. Most people in the world still do not have access to organised medical services. The search for alternative ways of improving health is not an interesting diversion for most of the world. It is an urgent and essential part of any attempt to enhance the basic welfare of women, men and children. It is therefore not surprising that many of the most impressive, the most thought-provoking and the most stimulating advances in theory and practice have come from work on health in the poor countries of the world.

An example from Brazil, reported by Brems (1984), serves to link the discussion of health with the previous discussion of women and welfare, and to put very specifically the relevance for social welfare policy and practice in the industrial world.

In 1982 the Institute of Cultural Action undertook a study to establish why local health and medical services were so little used by women in two *favelas* on the outskirts of the Brazilian city of Paraty. Women in those communities very clearly identified the problem; the services offered were not what they wanted:

Their chief concerns were:
— the deficiencies in the medical attention available to them; many perceived doctors as insensitive to women's needs.
— lack of knowledge about their own body and how it functions.
— depression and related mental health issues.
— the unsanitary conditions in which they lived [Brems, 1984: 15].

It is immediately striking how similar these responses are to those which have begun to dominate community health discussions in the rich countries. The fourth point is essentially similar to concerns with the effects, both physiological and psychological, of the environment.

The initial survey was followed up in discussion groups, which met every three weeks for a year. Participants found a number of common problems, among these were:

— Interpersonal relationships and sexuality.
— Economic dependence and day care.
— The need for a support network and for women to talk together.

— Appropriate pre-natal care and why it is important.
— The attitudes of health workers and the need for counselling on normal functions, not just illness.
— Consumers' rights in health services.
— The alienating policies of hospitals, particularly in childbirth and post-partum. One woman complained that 'women are taught to be mothers, but not to give birth'.
— Maternity leave and post-natal care.
— The breakdown in the family and community support network brought about by increased in-hospital births. Hospitals vs. traditional birth attendants.
— Preventive health and knowing your own body [Brems, 1984: 15].

Again, the familiarity of these issues to those engaged in similar work in the industrial countries is dramatic. Brems concluded that the project 'again confirms that a person's health is the result of a diverse set of conditions that contribute to well-being' (p. 16). This is relevant in all communities, in all countries; how relevant is Brems's final thought?

Most of all, the project demonstrates that people need to be able to find a time and space to reflect on themselves and their lives. The women of the favelas of Paraty have taught this and, in the process, are learning how to live better [p. 16].

Essentially the same issues appear in one of the best recent reviews of primary health care in action. Morley *et al.* identify two basic criteria for the assessment of programme success: *medical effectiveness* and *social impact* (Morley *et al.*, 1983: 319). They emphasise the role of women in particular. Muller, in the same volume, describes programmes in Peru; he argues that the nature of partici-pation is fundamental. 'Community participation', he suggests, should not be interpreted as merely the *mobilis-ation* of human and material resources. It should rather be understood as the community increasing its *control* over the social, political, economic and environmental factors affecting the health status of all its members: 'Social impact . . . is indicated by the community's increased awareness of health problems and capacity to organise itself to solve these problems' (Muller, 1983: 194).

Morley *et al.* conclude their assessment of case studies

from seventeen countries with recognition of 'two inte-
grating themes . . . the importance of political commitment
to equitable socioeconomic development, and the need for
community participation in planning, implementing and
evaluating PHC' (Morley *et al.*, 1983: 321).

In this aspect of policy responses to health needs we can
again see clear and direct links with contemporary issues in
the rich countries. These countries spend vastly more on
health services, perhaps forty times more per capita than the
poor countries. But there are doubts about the relationship
between more and more spending on health services and
the achievement of better health. Thus, as Townsend and
Davidson suggest:

'Development' in both kinds of country is increasingly recognised as
being a process which involves social and not just economic values, and
which, so far as the goal of good health is concerned, entails better
universal education, good conditions of work, good amenities in the
environment and in the home, well-integrated social services, and relatively high minimum living standards as well as reasonable standards of
medicine and nursing [Townsend and Davidson, 1982: 13].

Debates on health in the rich countries are increasingly
concerned with the medicalisation of health, the social
inequalities of both health conditions and responses to those
conditions, the social production of ill-health and the
political economy of health and illness. In all these, the
issues and the forms for their analysis are those which dominate discussion of policies for health in the poor countries.

In the UK, the Black Report (DHSS, 1981; Townsend
and Davidson, 1983) was an example of the approach. The
report was concerned with class inequalities in health, which
have shown no signs of narrowing despite enormous
increases in real expenditure over thirty years. It was a
powerful attempt to redirect medicine, and services for
health, towards a social concept of health and a social model
of health practice and action. The social bases of ill-health
were clearly identified; among the most important themes
in policy terms was emphasis on a total not merely service-
oriented approach to health. Many of the factors affecting
health were seen to lie outside the ambit of the organised

health services, and of national health policy. The social and economic factors affecting health were very heavily weighted against the lower social classes. Thus the report argued for changes within health services which would redress the balance of the health care system so that more emphasis be given to prevention, primary care, and community health. A basic unity of purpose, analysis and strategy can be seen in this report and in health work and health policy in poor countries. Work such as the Black Report is profoundly important insofar as it represents a coherent attempt to shift attention, in terms of actual practice, away from medical services rooted in and determined by the conventional medical model. It is vitally important that, as the WHO has urged world-wide, people should 'take more responsibility for their own health'. There needs to be recognition that how people 'live their lives is more important than any help from the health care system . . . an escape from medical dependency' (Abel-Smith, 1981: 96). But what happens within the health care system is vital, and just as in poor countries, emphasis is on *primary health care*. The rich countries have a great deal to learn about that from the successes and failures of the many countries in which primary health care programmes have been initiated and developed.

COMMUNITY DEVELOPMENT

The rich countries ignore virtually everything that has been achieved in the poor countries. Yet in the responses to welfare needs there are many instances of powerful advances, both in theory and practice. In relation to the elderly, to young offenders, the disabled, the care of children, the mentally ill, the illiterate, the dispossessed, the homeless, the workless and very many others, projects, programmes and approaches have been developed which transcend the constraints of orthodox welfare organisation and illustrate the infinite possibilities for genuine human welfare, altruism and imagination. The general neglect of this vast experience has been one theme of this book. The relative difficulty for interested people in rich countries to learn of such experience is but one result of structured dependence and 'professional imperialism'. Insularity, prejudice and ignorance are of course bound with each other in mutual reinforcement.

In this final section, some aspects of community development are discussed. This is an area where the global perspective is perhaps most fully developed and the linkages between issues in rich and poor countries most explicit. Throughout this book, a common theme in social welfare responses has been identified; in many different forms, community-based social programmes have been seen as vital in attempts to forge relevant social policies. In all sectors there are policies which claim to embody the principles of 'community development', whether 'self-help' housing, primary health care, literacy schemes, women's development projects or community-based social service schemes. If we look at what is commonly referred to as 'community development', we can begin to identify some common issues in what Marsden and Oakley have referred to as:

a host of, as yet, relatively uncoordinated efforts associated with a general movement for radical community action. This movement questions traditional, formal welfare strategies and parallels the development of similar courses of action in the UK and the USA [Marsden and Oakley, 1982: 161].

'Community development' has been used as a cloak to cover such a disparate set of approaches to social action that in practice the term has frequently been robbed of much of its meaning. The shift from colonial 'mass education', through use as 'a technique', to its emergence as a profession has been reviewed elsewhere (MacPherson, 1982). For some it is possible to produce an elaborate taxonomy, but only by removing all real meaning:

[Community development] is used as *process* with strategies ranging from imposition or manipulation to self-determination. It is used as a *program* ranging from economic development to social welfare, and under auspices ranging from governmental to voluntary organisations and groups. And it is conceived by some as a social *movement* and possibly an emerging *profession* [Popenhoe, 1967: 260].

There is in this no notion of the goals of development; the objective is essentially the achievement of 'a community' which functions more effectively; no *specific* objectives are at stake. The process of change is abstracted from its social and political context, and attention is diverted away from the significance of linkages which affect the quality of life, just as it is drawn away from attention on the quality of life itself, as the fundamental objective of development.

Those activities which are seen as comprising contemporary community development can only be understood in a radically different perspective. Community initiatives, across the whole range of concerns relevant to social welfare, vary enormously in style and content, but there are common elements. In the late 1970s and into the 1980s these elements have been seen to coalesce, and in particular around notions such as 'Another Development' (Wolfe, 1981: 241–65). With their emphasis on inequality and exploitation, in the context of national and international linkages, such approaches stress development itself as an objective and the potential power of people in communities. The romantic views of earlier periods are much more rare, however, as proponents of grass-roots community action identify the real nature of the task. For their discussion of community action, Marsden and Oakley take a conceptual framework elaborated by Galjart which he describes as 'counter-development':

This approach entails intervention to facilitate the effort of relatively small local groups in achieving, in a participatory manner, their development goals, and thus enhancing their members' life chances, in spite of, and in opposition to societal mechanisms and processes which influence these chances adversely [Galjart, 1981: 88].

The possibilities for such action are limited. Especially, but not only, in the case of government-sponsored programmes, there are very many cases in which a facade of commitment to participation has been shown to conceal the continuation of old patterns of exploitation and the establishment of new ones.

Wolfe (1981), in a powerful and wide-ranging discussion of development in global terms, draws especially on the

Latin American experience, and incisively lays bare the realities of 'aided self-help'. He argues that policy proposals incorporating aided self-help may be seen by their proponents as:

a potential means by which the 'critically poor' can raise levels of living without burdening the State with the very high costs of systems of assistentialism-cum-repression, and also without requiring an egalitarian revolutionary transformation—judged unattainable or unacceptable—in social and economic relationships [Wolfe, 1981: 234].

Such approaches, says Wolfe, must force the mass of poor people into a subordinate 'parallel economy' which both allows and enables the dynamic 'modern' sector to advance even more vigorously, freed of most of the costs and threats of mass 'critical poverty'. The poor majority must accept minimal improvements in their own conditions, but must work to support services that the state provides for others. Their willingness to do this, he argues, would be most likely to break down precisely when progress had generated hope and organisational capacity, unless there were yet more rigorous controls. He is scathing about aided self-help schemes as comprehensive solutions, when they can at best only bring secondary improvements for a minority of the poor.

Just as it is the forces of the social, political and economic context which so crucially shape the conditions of the poor, so is it these forces which constrain the potential of local community action beyond local communities:

The propensity to over-generalize about the potential of aided self-help and to assume that localized achievements can be duplicated on an ever-larger scale . . . has been particularly evident in the changing fashions for diagnoses and policy proposals for urban shanty-towns [Wolfe, 1981: 235].

Those who live in such settlements are not hopeless, unemployable migrants condemning themselves and their children to a perpetual 'culture of poverty'. Nor are they all, as some other generalisations would suggest, dynamic, creative and energetic people who can be left to solve their own problems with very little outside aid and minimal interference. Settlements vary enormously, not just in their physical conditions but in the degrees of dynamism, creativity and energy that are present. But even when these are there to be harnessed for development, the realities of the wider context must temper the more sweeping assumptions about the potential for local action:

At best they confront formidable constraints from the wider urban and national society. They cannot enable the families concerned to extricate themselves from the costs of urban sprawl and the polluted urban environment to that which the settlements contribute, nor to compete on equitable terms in the job market and the educational system that helps to determine access to jobs [Wolfe, 1981: 236].

But although the constraints on community action are immense, the significance of the innumerable examples of such action is very great indeed. What is vital is a recognition of the contradictions highlighted by these actions. In terms of a global perspective on welfare, if these small-scale actions are seen in context, then 'the conflict between rich and poor takes on international dimensions as the boundaries which supported the "independent" nation state are called into question and those boundaries which separate rich and poor are increasingly de-mystified' (Marsden and Oakley, 1982: 161). As suggested so often in this book, the linkages which affect welfare in both the rich and the poor countries are international as well as national; so too is the essential nature of welfare and human development. As Shirley remarks, in a discussion of community development as 'critical practice', 'the task of the development agent is to continually translate personal troubles into public issues and public issues into terms of their human meaning' (Shirley, 1982: 267). This is ultimately the purpose of social welfare policy and practice in every country, however rich or however poor.

In practice, the possibilities for welfare policies and programmes informed by a concern with community action are extremely limited. The mass of people, in all countries, are preoccupied by immediate problems of security and livelihood. We may see, in very many different settings, a search for meaning in social events; a concern for something more satisfying than a ceaseless struggle to make ends meet. But we are all selective in our perceptions, and there is a great danger of assuming that values and aspirations are commonly shared, or of ignoring the realities of conflicting interests.

But, nonetheless, there can be no doubt that the actions of many hundreds of thousands of communities have demonstrated the strength of community actions for welfare. It is also the case that their linkages are becoming clearer.

The most consistent, coherent and compelling conceptual framework for understanding those linkages is that of *self-reliance*. The emergence of this, as a reaction to the perverted economic and social development of the postwar period, was associated particularly with Julius Nyerere of Tanzania (MacPherson, 1982). But it has, in the past twenty years, gained widespread support. It is as far from notions of individualism and self-interest as can be imagined. It is, as a basis for development, essentially the dialectical product of its opposite in the economic and social patterns forced on poor countries. As a focus for radical criticism of these patterns and their inherent relationships, 'self-reliance' highlights 'parallels between the international, the national, local-community, and the family-individual spheres of action and interaction' (Wolfe, 1981: 263); not least because they are essentially concerned with relationships of dominance and dependence. These relationships have become frustrating for dominant forces in rich as well as poor countries. The threats of ever-rising indebtedness, the activities of transnational corporations and the repeated crises which have resulted from the economic and political rivalry of major world powers, have led many states to seek more autonomy—if only to increase their bargaining power.

At the same time, developmentalist-welfare states are unable to satisfy all the demands made on them. This has caused national political leaderships to divest the state of some of its responsibilities through controlled decentralis-ation, privatisation or other means. A host of criticisms are directed at the state, from very different directions: criti-cisms of its insatiable fiscal appetites, its paternalism, bureaucracy, failure to address social problems, inability to provide efficient services or enough jobs. In rich and poor countries alike, frustrations and fears have revived very diverse ideological and religious forces. For equally diverse reasons these reject centralisation, regimentation, paternalism, assistentialism, mass-consumption society and other aspects of contemporary societies contrary to self-reliance and self-sufficiency. As we have seen, the forces of dependence and domination reach throughout national societies, both poor and rich, to the level of households, families and relationships. To a very great extent, emphasis on self-reliance expresses precisely that conjunction of economic and personal dimensions alluded to in earlier discussions of welfare in a development perspective. But although awareness of these issues has grown and is now reflected in analysis and practice, so too have the forces acting against self-reliance. The strength of those forces creating and recreating national entanglement in the web of dependence has not diminished. Nor has that of the forces which entangle individuals, families and communities in 'the web of techno-bureaucracy' (Wolfe, 1981: 264).

Self-reliance may be seen as at the heart of much that is positive in the welfare gains which have been made in the context of development. This goes far beyond immediate issues of resources to questions of individual welfare. But in doing so it must relate outwards to the wider context—economic, social and political. Much of what has been outlined in this book has this concept as its key. If welfare is the development of people, as individuals and as social beings, aiming at liberation and fulfilment, it cannot come from anywhere but the inner core of each society:

It relies on what a human group has: its natural environment, its cultural heritage, the creativity of the men and women who constitute it, becoming richer through exchange between them and with other groups. It entails the autonomous definition of development styles and of life styles . . . it does not ask the question 'how much can we get through exchange', but 'how much can we produce ourselves or with others'. Thus, the basis is laid for a search for new resources, for utilising known resources in new ways and sometimes for questioning the need for the product . . . A self-reliant society is able to stand up better to crises: it is self-confident and has the means to sustain its dignity [Dag Hammarskjöld Foundation, 1975: 34–5].

Our principal purpose has been to indicate the importance of a global perspective. We are doing little more than C. Wright Mills did so much more eloquently in his case for the 'sociological imagination'. The social analyst with such imagination asked three sorts of questions: those to do with social structure, those to do with development and those to do with human nature (Wright Mills, 1970: 13). What more, or less, are we concerned to ask? We have put the case, and attempted to illustrate it, for asking these questions in relation to welfare, and for doing so in ways which break through the present divisions of interest in welfare:

For that imagination is the capacity to shift from one perspective to another—from the political to the psychological; from the examination of a single family to comparative assessment of the national budgets of the world . . . it is the capacity to range from the most impersonal and remote transformations to the most intimate features of the human self—and to see the relations between the two . . . Older decisions that once appeared sound, now seem . . . products of a mind unaccountably dense . . . [the] capacity for astonishment is made lively again [Wright Mills, 1970: 13–14].

Bibliography

Aaron, H. (1967) 'Social security: international comparisons' in O. Eckstein (ed.), pp. 13–48.

Abel-Smith, B. (1981) 'Towards a healthier population', *New Society*, 15 October 1981, pp. 95–7.

Abel-Smith, B. and Leiserson, A. (1978) *Poverty, Development and Health Policy*, Public Health Paper, No. 69, Geneva: World Health Organisation.

Abhu-Lughod, J. and Hay, R. (eds.) (1979) *Third World Urbanisation*, London: Methuen.

Acosta, C. J. (1976) 'Columbian élites and the Underdevelopment of the Social Welfare System', in D. Thursz and J. L. Vigilante (eds), vol. 2, pp. 221–40.

Adelman, I. and Morris, C. T. (1973) *Economic Growth and Social Equity in Developing Countries*, Stanford: Stanford University Press.

Adler, Z. and Midgley, J. (1984) 'Social work education in developing countries', *Social Word Today*, 48, 16–17.

Ahluwalia, M. (1974) 'Income inequality: some discussions of the problems' in H. Chenery *et al.* (eds.), *Redistribution with Growth*, pp. 3–37.

Ahluwalia, M. (1976) 'Inequality, poverty and development', *Journal of Development Economics* 3, 307–42.

Ahluwalia, M. *et al.* (1978) *Growth and Poverty in Developing Countries*, Washington: World Bank.

Amin, S. (1974) *Accumulation on a World Scale*, New York: Monthly Review.

Amin, S. (1976) *Unequal Development*, Brighton: Harvester.

Anand, A. (1980) *Rethinking Women and Development: The Case for Feminism*,

Anand, A. (1985) 'Our day has begun', *Development Forum*, 13 (7), 1, 14.

Aptekar, H. (1965) 'Social work in cross-cultural perspective' in S. K. Khinduka (ed.), pp. 117–36.

Apthorpe, R. (ed.) (1970) *People, Planning and Development Studies*, London: Cass.

Azicri, M. (1980) 'Cuban family code: some observations on its innovations and continuities', *Review of Socialist Law* 6, 183–91.

Baig, T. A. (1979) 'Overview of child welfare' in India, Ministry of Social Welfare, *Profile of the Child in India*, New Delhi: Ministry of Social Welfare.

Bairoch, P. (1975) *The Economic Development of the Third World Since 1900*, London: Methuen.

Baker, J. (1979) 'Social conscience and social policy', *Journal of Social Policy* (2), 177–206.

Bakker, M. L. (1984) *Spatial Differentiation of Mortality in Papua New Guinea*, Census Working Paper No. 4, Port Moresby: PNG Bureau of Statistics.

Ballard, J. A. (1981) *Policy-Making in a New State*, St Lucia: University of Queensland Press.

Baster, N. (ed.) (1972) *Measuring Development*, London: Frank Cass.

Baster, N. (1985) 'Social indicator research' in J. Hilhorst and M. Klatter (eds.), pp. 23–46.

Bedi, M. S. (1978) *Socially Handicapped Children: A Study of Their Institutional Services*, Jodhpur: Jain.

Bennett, F. J. (1979) 'Primary health care and developing countries', *Social Science and Medicine* 13A, 505–14.

Benyoussef, A. and Christian, B. (1977) 'Health care in developing countries', *Social Science and Medicine* 11 (6/7), 399–408.

Blunt, E. (ed.) (1938) *Social Service in India*, London: HMSO.

Boahen, A. A. (ed.) (1984) *Africa under Foreign Domination, 1880–1935*. (General History of Africa, Vol. VII), London: UNESCO; Heinemann and University of California Press.

Bossert, T. *et al.* (1984) 'The political and administrative cost of primary health care in the Third World', *Social Science and Medicine* 18 (8), 693–702.

Bradshaw, J. (1972) 'The concept of social need', *New Society* 30, 640–3.

Brandt, W. *et al.* (1980) *North–South: A Programme for Survival*, London: Pan.

Brems, S. (1984) 'Brazil: learning to live better', *Contact* 80, August, 15–16.

Bridgland, K. (1972) 'Mobile crèches in India: a new basis for community development in Delhi', *Community Development Journal*, April, 136–41.

Brokensha, D. and Hodge, P. (1969) *Community Development: An Interpretation*, San Francisco: Chandler.

Caplan, P. (1985) 'Womens voluntary social welfare work in India: the cultural construction of gender and class, *Bulletin of Concerned Asian Scholars* 17 (1) 20–31.

Carrier, J. and Kendall, I. (1973) Social Policy and Social Change: Explanations of the Development of Social Policy, *Journal of Social Policy* 2 (3), 209–24.

Carrier, J. and Kendall, I. (1977) 'The development of welfare states: the production of plausible accounts', *Journal of Social Policy* 6 (3), 271–90.

Cesaire, A. (1972) *Discourse on Colonialism*, New York: Monthly Review Press.

Chambers, R. (1984) *Rural Development: Putting the Last First*, London: Longman.

Chambliss, R. (1954) *Social Thought*, New York: Holt, Rinehard & Winston.

Chaturvedi, T. N. (ed.) (1979) *Administration for Child Welfare*, New Delhi: Indian Institute of Public Administration.

Chenery, H. *et al.* (1974) *Redistribution with Growth*, London: Oxford University Press.

Chenery, H. and Syrquin, M. (1975) *Patterns of Development 1950–1970*, London: Oxford University Press.

Chowning, A. (1977) *An Introduction to the Peoples and Cultures of Melanesia*, Menlo Park, California: Cummings.

Cockburn, C. (1980) 'The role of social security in development', *International Social Security Revew* 33 (3), 337–58.

Constantine, D. (1984) *British Colonial Development Policy, 1914–1940*, London: Cass.

Constantino, R. (1977) *Philippines: A Past Revisited*, New York: Monthly Review Press.

Conyers, D. (1982) *An Introduction to Social Planning in the Third World*, Chichester: Wiley.

Cumper, G. (1972) *Survey of Social Legislation in Jamaica*, Mona: University of the West Indies Institute for Social and Economic Research.

Cutright, P. (1965) 'Political structure, economic development and social security programs', *American Journal of Sociology* 70, 537–50.

D'Aeth, R. (1975) *Education and Development in the Third World*, Farnborough: Saxon House.

Dag Hammarskjöld Foundation (1975) *What Now? Another Development*, Uppsala: Dag Hammarskjöld Foundation.

Davidson, B. (1967) *The Growth of African Civilisation*, London: Longman.

Davidson, B. (1984) *The Story of Africa*, London: BBC Publications.

Deacon, B. (1983) *Social Policy and Socialism*, London: Pluto.

Deuschle, K. W. (1982) 'Community oriented primary care: lessons learned in three decades', *Journal of Community Health* 8 (1), 13–22.

D.H.S.S. (1981) *Inequalities in Health: Report of a Research Working Group* (The Black Report), London: Department of Health and Social Security.

Dixon, J. (1981) *The Chinese Welfare System 1949–1979*, New York: Praeger.

Djeudjang, G-L. (1977) 'L'enfant devant la justice au Cameroun', *Revue Juridique et Politique – Indépendance et Coopération* 31 (2), 168–250.

Djukanovic, V. and Mach, E. P. (1975) *Alternative Approaches to Meeting Basic Health Needs in Developing Countries*, Geneva: World Health Organisation.

Dore, R. (1976) *The Diploma Disease*, London: Allen and Unwin.

Doyal, L. and Pennell, I. (1979) *The Political Economy of Health*, London: Pluto.

Drakakis-Smith, D. (1981) *Housing, Urbanization and the Development Process*, London: Croom Helm.

Drewnowski, J. (1970) *Studies in the Measurement of Levels of Living and Welfare*, Geneva: United Nations Research Institute for Social Development.

Dubey, S. N. (1973) *Administration of Welfare Programmes in India*, Bombay: Somaiya.

de Duran, S. M. (1983) 'Child legislation in Colombia', in A. M. Pappas (ed.), *Law and the Status of the Child*, New York: UNITAR, pp. 101–82.

Eckstein, O. (ed.) (1967) *Studies in the Economics of Income Maintenance*, Washington: Brookings.

Elogo, (1980) 'Recent developments and future prospects of social security in French-speaking Africa', *Social Security Document-ation* 3, 31–71.

Emmanuel, A. (1974) *Unequal Exchange*, New York: Monthly Review Press.

Estes, R. J. (1984) *The Social Progress of Nations*, New York: Praeger.

F.A.O. *See* Food and Agricultural Organisation.

Fanon, F. (1967) *The Wretched of the Earth*, Harmondsworth: Penguin.

Feacham, R. *et al.* (1977) *Water Wastes and Health in Hot Climates*, London: Wiley.

Fields, G. S. (1980) *Poverty, Inequality and Development*, Cambridge: Cambridge University Press.

Finlay, O. (1983) 'The rights of children in Cuba', in A. M. Pappas (ed.), *Law and the Status of the Child*, 221–62, New York: UNITAR.

Fisher, P. (1968) 'Social security and development planning', in E. M. Kassalow (ed.), pp. 239–61.

Food and Agricultural Organization (1974) *World Food Conference*, Rome: FAO.

Food and Agricultural Organization (1975) *The State of Food and Agriculture 1974*, Rome: FAO.

Forder, A. (1974) *Concepts in Social Administration*, London: Routledge & Kegan Paul.

Foster, P. (1965) *Education and Social Change in Ghana*, London: Routledge & Kegan Paul.

Fox, M. G. (1976) *Social Welfare Services and Development Planning in the Pacific Islands*, Noumea: South Pacific Commission.

Frank, A. G. (1967) *Capitalism and Underdevelopment in Latin America*, New York: Monthly Review Press.

Froland, C. *et al.* (1981) *Helping Networks and Human Services*, Beverly Hills: Sage.

Galenson, W. (1968) 'A quantitative approach to social security and economic development' in E. M. Kassalow (ed.), pp. 51–66.

Galjart, B. (1981) 'Counterdevelopment: a position paper', *Community Development Journal* 16 (2), 88–96.

Gangrade, K. D. (ed.) (1978) *Social Legislation in India*, (2 vols), Delhi: Concept.

George, V. and Wilding, P. (1984) *The Impact of Social Policy*, London: Routledge & Kegan Paul.

Gilbert, N. (1976) 'Alternative forms of social protection for developing countries', *Social Service Review* 50, 363–87.

Ginsburg, N. (1979) *Class, Capital and Social Policy*, London: Macmillan.

Gish, O. (1977) *Guidelines for Health Planners*, London: Tri-Med.

Gish, O. (1979) 'The political economy of primary care and "health by the people": an historical explanation', *Social Science and Medicine*, 13c (4), 203–11.

Gish, O. (1983) 'Some observations about health development in three African socialist countries: Ethiopia, Mozambique and Tanzania', *Social Science and Medicine* 17 (24), 1961–9.

Gokhale, S. D. (ed.) (1975) *Social Welfare: Legend and Legacy*, Bombay: Prakashan.

Gokhale, S. D. and Sohoni, N. K. (eds.) (1979) *Child in India*, Bombay: Somaiya.

Goldthorpe, J. H. (1962) 'Development of social policy in England, 1800–1914' in International Sociological Association, *Transactions of the Fifth World Congress of Sociology*, Washington, pp. 42–50.

Golladay, F. (1980) *Health Problems and Policies in the Developing Countries*, Washington: World Bank.

Gordon, M. (1963) *The Economics of Welfare Policies*, New York: Columbia University Press.

Gough, I. (1979) *The Political Economy of the Welfare State*, London: Macmillan.

Gray, N. and Daube, M. (1980) *Guidelines for Smoking Control*, Geneva: International Union Against Cancer.

Gruat, (1984) 'The extension of social protection in the Gabonese Republic', *International Labour Review* 123 (4): 457–72.

Hall, P. *et al.* (1975) *Change, Choice and Conflict in Social Policy*, London: Heinemann.

Hallen, G. C. (1967) *Social Security in India*, Meerut: Rastogi.

Hardiman, M. and Midgley, J. (1978) 'Foreign consultants and development projects: the need for an alternative approach', *Journal of Administration Overseas* 17, 155–65.

Hardiman, M. and Midgley, J. (1980) 'Training social planners for social development, *Internation Social Work*, 23, 1–14.

Hardiman, M. and Midgley, J. (1981) 'Planning and the health of mothers and children in the rural areas of Sierra Leone', *Journal of Tropical Pediatrics* 27, 83–7.

Hardiman, M. and Midgley, J. (1982a) *The Social Dimensions of Development: Social Policy and Planning in the Third World*, Chichester: Wiley.

Hardiman, M. and Midgley, J. (1982b) 'Social planning and access to the social services in developing countries', *Third World Planning Review* 4, 74–86.

Hay, J. R. (1975) *The Origins of the Liberal Welfare Reforms*, London: Macmillan.

Hayter, T. (1971) *Aid as Imperialism*, Harmondsworth: Penguin.

Heclo, H. (1974) *Modern Social Policies in Britain and Sweden*, New Haven: Yale University Press.

Heidenheimer, A. *et al.* (1975) *Comparative Public Policy*, New York: St Martins.

Heisler, H. (1967) 'Social service in Africa: Western approaches', *Social and Economic Administration* 1, 56–69.

Higgins, J. (1979) 'Social control theories of social policy', *Journal of Social Policy* 9, 1–23.

Higgins, J. (1981) *States of Welfare: Comparative Analysis in Social Policy*, Oxford: Blackwell and Robertson.

Hilhorst, J. and Klatter, M. (eds.) (1985) *Social Development in the Third World*, London: Croom Helm.

Hodge, P. (1973) 'Social policy: an historical perspective as seen in colonial policy', *Journal of Oriental Studies* 11 (2), 207–19.

Hodge, P. (ed.) (1980) *Culture and Social Work: Education and Practice in South East Asia*, Hong Kong: Heinemann.

Hopkins, M. (1982) 'A global forecast of absolute poverty and employment', *International Labour Review* 119, 565–77.

Huston, P. (1979) *Third World Women Speak Out*, New York: Praeger.

Hyden, G. (1980) *Beyond Ujamaa in Tanzania*, London: Heinemann.

Ijere, M. (1966) 'Indigenous African social security as a basis for future planning: the case of Nigeria', *Bulletin of the International Social Security Association* 11 (12), 463–87.

I.L.O. (1942) *Approaches to Social Security: An International Survey*, Geneva: International Labour Office.

I.L.O. (1976) *Employment, Growth and Basic Needs: A One World Problem*, Geneva: International Labour Organisation.

I.L.O. (1982) *ILO/Norway Regional Training Course on Social Security in Africa*, Geneva: International Labour Organisation.

India, Central Social Welfare Board (1974) *Orphanages in India: A Study*, New Delhi: CSWB.

India, Department of Social Welfare (1975) *Integrated Child Development Services Scheme*, New Delhi.

I.S.S.A. (1982) 'Social security and the elderly: background document prepared for the World Assembly on Aging by the International Social Security Association, *International Social Security Review* 35, 489–529.

Jacob, A. (1979) 'Neglected children and the law', in A. de Souza (ed.)

Jain, S. N. and Loghani, V. (eds.) (1979) *Child and the Law*, New Delhi: Indian Law Institute.

Johri, C. K. and Schri, R. (1982) 'Social security in India: issues and prospects', *Labour and Society* 2, 105–20.

Jones, H. (1983) 'Some factors in Third World social policy', *Social Policy and Administration* 17 (2), 106–17.

Karl, M. (1984) 'Introduction to special issue on rural women', *Ideas and Action* 158, 2–3.

Kassalow, E. M. (ed.) (1968) *The Role of Social Security in Economic Development*, Washington: US Dept. of Health, Education and Welfare.

Kayongo-Male, D. and Onyanago, P. (1984) *Sociology of the African Family*, London: Longman.

Kerr, C. *et al.* (1973) *Industrialism and Industrial Man*, Harmondsworth: Penguin.

Khandekar, M. (1979) *Planning Integrated Services for Urban Children and Youth*, Bombay: Tata Institute.

Khinduka, S. K. (ed.) (1965) *Social Work in India*, Allahabad: Kitab Mahal.

Kilby, P. and Taira, K. (1969) 'Differences in social security development in selected countries', *International Social Security Review* 22, 139–54.

Kitching, G. (1982) *Development and Underdevelopment in Historical Perspective*, London: Methuen.

Kravis, I. B. (1960) 'International differences in the distribution of income', *Review of Economics and Statistics* 42, 408–16.

Kulkarni, V. M. (1979) *Essays in Social Administration*, Delhi: Research Publications in Social Sciences.

Kuznets, S. (1955) 'Economic growth and income inequality', *American Economic Review* 45, 1–28.

Kuznets, S. (1963) 'Quantitative aspects of economic growth of nations III, Distribution of Income by Size', *Economic Development and Cultural Change* 11, 1–80.

Lachenmann, G. (1982) *Primary Health Care and Basic Needs Orientation in Developing Countries*, Berlin: German Development Institute.

Lalitha, N. V. (1977) *Foster Care Services in India: A Study*, New Delhi: National Institute of Public Cooperation and Child Development.

Landa-Jocano, F. (1980) *Social Work in the Philippines*, Manila: New Day Publishers.

Le Grand, J. (1982) *The Strategy of Equality*, London: Allen & Unwin.

Levine, H. B. and Levine, M. W. (1979) *Urbanisation in Papua New Guinea*, London: Cambridge University Press.

Lewis, O. (1966) 'The culture of poverty', *Scientific American* 214, 19–25.

Leys, C. (1975) *Underdevelopment in Kenya*, London: Heinemann.

Lipton, M. (1977) *Why Poor People Stay Poor*, London: Temple Smith.

Livingstone, A. (1969) *Social Policy in Developing Countries*, London: Routledge & Kegan Paul.

Lloyd, P. (1979) *Slums of Hope?*, Harmondsworth: Penguin.

Long, N. (1977) *An Introduction to the Sociology of Rural Development*, London: Tavistock.

Loup, J. (1983) *Can the Third World Survive?* Baltimore: Johns Hopkins University Press.

MacGranahan, D. V. (1970) *Content and Measurement of Socio-Economic Development*, Geneva: United Nations Research Institute for Social Development.

Macnaught, T. J. (1976) *The Fijian Colonial Experience*, Canberra: Australian National University.

MacNamara, R. (1973) *Address to the Board of Governors*, Washington: World Bank.

MacPherson, S. (1980) 'Development of basic health services in Papua New Guinea', PhD thesis, University of Nottingham.

MacPherson, S. (1981) 'Basic health services in Papua New Guinea' in Z. Mars (ed.) *Organising for Health*, Brighton: Institute of Development Studies.

MacPherson, S. (1982) *Social Policy in the Third World: The Social Dilemmas of Underdevelopment*, Brighton: Harvester.

MacPherson, S. (1983) 'The underdevelopment of social administration' in P. T. Bean and S. MacPherson (eds.) *Approaches to Welfare*, London: Routledge & Kegan Paul.

MacPherson, S. (1985) *Legislation and Child Welfare*, Geneva: World Health Organisation.

MacPherson, S. (1987a) *500 Million Children: Child Welfare in the Third World*, Brighton: Wheatsheaf.

MacPherson, S. (1987b) 'Social security and social assistance in developing countries', *Social Policy and Administration*, forthcoming.

Madison, B. (1980) *The Meaning of Social Policy: The Comparative Dimension in Social Welfare*, London: Croom Helm.

Mahadevan, M. (1977) 'Mobile crèches in India', *Assignment Children*, 31, 124–129.

Mair, L. (1944) *Welfare in the British Colonies*, London: Royal Institute of International Affairs.

Mair, L. (1984) *Anthropology and Development*, London: Macmillan.

Mallett, A. (1980) 'Social protection of the rural population', *International Social Security Review*, 3 (4), 359–93.

Malloy, J. (1979) *The Politics of Social Security in Brazil*, Pittsburgh: University of Pittsburgh Press.

Maloney, K. (1986) 'More than a parley', *Community Development Journal*, 21 (1), January, 52–8.

Mamdani, M. (1976) *Politics and Class Formation in Uganda*, New York: Monthly Review Press.

Marsden, D. and Oakley, P. (1982) 'Radical community development in the Third World' in G. Craig *et al.* (eds.), *Community Work and the State*, London: Routledge & Kegan Paul.

Mburu, F. M. (1983) 'Health systems as defences against the consequences of poverty: equity in health as social justice', *Social Science and Medicine*, 17 (16), 1149–57.

Melrose, D. (1982) *Bitter Pills*, Oxford: Oxfam.

Mesa-Lago, C. (1978) *Social Security in Latin America*, Pittsburgh: University of Pittsburgh Press.

Mesa-Lago, C. (1983) 'Social security and extreme poverty in Latin America', *Journal of Development Economics* 12, 83–110.

Midgley, J. (1981) *Professional Imperialism: Social Work in the Third World*, London: Heinemann.

Midgley, J. (1984a) *Social Security, Inequality and the Third World*, Chichester: Wiley.

Midgley, J. (1984b) 'Diffusion and the development of social policy: evidence from the Third World', *Journal of Social Policy* 13, 167–84.

Midgley, J. (1984c) 'Poor law principles and social assistance in the Third World: a study of the perpetuation of colonial welfare', *International Social Work* 27, 2–12.

Midgley, J. (1984d) 'Social welfare implications of development paradigms', *Social Service Review* 58, 181–98.

Midgley, J. (1984e) 'Fields of practice and professional roles for social planners: an overview' in J. Midgley and D. Piachaud (eds.), pp. 11–33.

Midgley, J. and Hamilton, D. (1978) 'Local initiative and the role of community development: policy implications of a study in Sierra Leone', *International Social Work* 21, 2–11.

Midgley, J. and Piachaud, D. (1984) 'Social indicators and social planning', in J. Midgley and D. Piachaud (eds.), pp. 34–55.

Midgley, J. and Piachaud, D. (eds.) (1984) *The Fields and Methods of Social Planning*, London: Heinemann.

Mishra, R. (1977) *Society and Social Policy*, London: Macmillan.

Montas, H. P. (1983) 'Problems and perspectives in the financing of social security in Latin America', *International Social Security Review* 1, 70–87.

Morawetz, D. (1977) *Twenty-Five Years of Economic Development 1950 to 1975*, Baltimore: Johns Hopkins University Press.

Morgan, R. (ed.) (1984) *Sisterhood is Global*, Harmondsworth: Penguin.

Morley, D. *et al.* (1983) *Practising Health for All*, Oxford: Oxford University Press.

Morris, M. D. (1979) *Measuring the Conditions of the World's Poor*, New York: Pergamon.

Morsy, M. (1984) *North Africa 1800–1900: A Survey from the Nile Valley to the Atlantic*, London: Longman.

Moumouni, A. (1968) *Education in Africa*, London: Deutsch.

Mouton, P. (1975) *Social Security in Africa: Trends, Problems and Prospects*, Geneva: International Labour Organisation.

Muller, F. (1983) 'Contrasts in community participation: case studies from Peru' in D. Morley *et al.* (eds.) *Practising Health for All*, Oxford: Oxford University Press.

Muller, M. (1978) *Tobacco and the Third World: Tomorrows Epidemic?*, London: War on Want.

Muller, M. (1982) *The Health of Nations*, London: Faber.

Murison, H. S. and Lea, J. P. (eds.) (1979) *Housing in Third World Countries*, London: Macmillan.

Musiga, A. (1980) 'Recent developments and future prospects of social security in English-speaking Africa', *Social Security Documentation* 3, 21–9.

Nair, G. R. (1980) 'Towards social security: building a welfare society brick by brick, *Social Welfare* 5 (6), 71–4.

Navarro, V. (1974) 'The underdevelopment of health or the health of underdevelopment', *International Journal of Health Services* 4, 5–27.

Navarro, V. (1984) 'A critique of the ideological and political position of the Brandt Report and the Alma Ata Declaration', *International Journal of Health Services* 14 (2), 159–72.

Nelson, N. (1986) 'The end of the decade—or the beginning

for women? *Community Development Journal* 21 (1), January, 43–51.

Newell, K. W. (ed.) (1975) *Health by the People*, Geneva: World Health Organisation.

Onokerhoraye, A. G. (1984) *Social Services in Nigeria*, London: Routledge & Kegan Paul.

Open University (1985) *Health of Nations*, Milton Keynes: Open University Press.

Oshima, H. (1962) 'The international comparison of size distribution of family incomes with specific reference to Asia', *Review of Economics and Statistics* 44, 439–45.

Palma, G. (1981) 'Dependency and development: a critical overview' in D. Seers (ed.), pp. 20–78.

Palmer, I. (1980) 'Women in rural development', *International Development Review*, 22 (2–3), 39–45.

Pappas, A. M. (ed.) (1983) *Law and Status of the Child*, New York: Unitar.

Papua New Guinea: National Youth Movement (1981) *NYM Trainers Manual*, Port Moresby: NYM.

Piachaud, D. (1979) 'Inequality and social policy', *New Society* 47, 670–2.

Pinker, R. (1971) *Social Theory and Social Policy*, London: Heinemann.

Pinker, R. (1979) *The Idea of Welfare*, London: Heinemann.

Pinker, R. (1984) 'Populism and the social services', *Social Policy and Administration* 18, 89–99.

Piven, F. and Cloward, R. (1971) *Regulating the Poor: The Functions of Public Welfare*, New York: Pantheon.

Popenhoe, D. (1967) 'Community development and community planning', *Journal of the American Institute of Planners* 33, 259–65.

Population Information Program (1979) *Tobacco: Hazards to Health and Human Reproduction*, Baltimore: John Hopkins University.

Power, J. and Holenstein, A. (1976) *World of Hunger*, London: Temple Smith.

Prigmore, C. (1976) *Social Work in Iran since the White Revolution*, Alabama: University of Alabama Press.

Pryor, F. (1968) *Public Expenditure in Communist and Capitalist Nations*, Homewood: Irwin.

Ranger, T. O. (1969) *Colonialism in Africa 1870–1960*, Cambridge: Cambridge University Press.

Rao, S. V. (1979) 'Laws relating to children' in T. Chaturvedi (ed.). pp. 93–100.

Reidy, E. (1980) 'Welfarists and the market: a study of the self-employment assistance programme in the Philippines', *Development and Change* 11, 29–312.

Reutlinger, S. and Selowsky, M. (1976) *Malnutrition and Poverty*, Baltimore: John Hopkins University Press.

Rifkin, S. B. (1981) 'Health, political will and participation', *UNICEF News*, 108/81/2, pp. 3–5.

Rifkin, S. B. (1983) 'Primary health care in S. E. Asia: attitudes about community participation in community health programmes', *Social Science and Medicine* 17 (19), 1489–98.

Rimlinger, G. V. (1968) 'Social security and industrialization' in Kassalow, E. M. (ed.) pp. 129–54.

Rimlinger, G. V. (1971) *Welfare Policy and Industrialization in Europe, America and Russia*, New York: Wiley.

Rodgers, B. *et al.* (1968) *Comparative Social Administration*, London: Allen & Unwin.

Rodgers, B. *et al.* (1979) *The Study of Social Policy: A Comparative Approach*, London: Allen & Unwin.

Rodney, W. (1972) *How Europe Underdeveloped Africa*, Dar es Salaam: Tanzania Publishing House.

Rodriguez, S. L. E. (1976) 'Panama: social services, public and private' in D. Thursz, and J. L. Vigilante (eds.), vol. 2, pp. 265–72.

Roemer, R. (1982) *Legislative Action to Combat the World Smoking Epidemic*, Geneva: World Health Organisation.

Rogers, B. (1980) *The Domestication of Women*, London: Kogan Page.

Rohde, J. E. (1983) 'Oral rehydration therapy in UNICEF', *The State of the World's Children*, Oxford: Oxford University Press, pp. 72–7.

Rolt, F. (1985) *Pills, Policies and Profits*, London: War on Want.

Romero, F. R. P. (1979) 'Law in the world of the child', *Philippine Law Journal* 54, 277–312.

Roodkowsky, M. (1983) 'Women and development: a survey of the literature' in *Women in Development*, Geneva: ISIS.

Rosenstein-Rodan, P. (1961) 'International aid for underdeveloped countries', *Review of Economics and Statistics* 43, 107–38.

Rwezaura, B. A. (1977) 'Social fatherhood at the crossroads: a study of changes in child law in Tanzania', *East African Law Review* 10, 67–99.

Rys, V. (1964) 'The sociology of social security', *Bulletin of the ISSA*, Year 17, Nos. 1 and 2, pp. 3–34.

Sachs, I. (1982) 'Crisis of the welfare state and the exercise of social rights to development', *International Social Science Journal*, 34, 133–48.

Saunders, R. and Warford, J. (1976) *Village Water Supply*, Baltimore: Johns Hopkins University Press.

Seabrook, J. (1984) *Landscapes of Poverty*, London: Blackwell.

Seers, D. (ed.) (1981) *Dependency Theory: A Critical Re-assessment*, London: Pinter.

Segall, M. (1983) 'Planning and politics of resource allocation for primary health care: promotion of meaningful national policy', *Social Science and Medicine*, 17 (24), 1947–60.

Semmel, B. (1960) *Imperialism and Social Reform*, London: Allen and Unwin.

Shirley, I. (ed.) (1982) *Development Tracks: The Theory and Practice of Community Development*, Palmerstone North: The Dunmore Press.

Simey, T. (1946) *Welfare and Planning in the West Indies*, Oxford: Clarendon Press.

Singh, D. (1979) 'Mobile crèches' in India, Ministry of Social Welfare, *Profile of the Child in India*, Delhi: Ministry of Social Welfare, pp. 358–68.

Smith, A. D. (1979) *Nationalism in the Twentieth Century*, Oxford: Robertson.

Smith, A. D. (1981) *The Ethnic Revival*, Cambridge: Cambridge University Press.

de Souza, A. (ed.) (1979) *Children in India*, Delhi: Manohar.

Streeten, P. *et al.* (1981) *First Things First*, New York: Oxford University Press.

Stren, R. E. (1975) *Urban Inequality and Urban Housing Policy in Tanzania*, Berkeley: University of California Press.

Tawney, R. H. (1938) *The Acquisitive Society*, West Drayton: Penguin.

Tawney, R. (1936) *Religion and the Rise of Capitalism*, London: Murray.

Taylor, D. (1985) *Women: A World Report*, London: Methuen.

Tchibinda, J. F. and Mayetela, N. (1983) 'The rights of the child in the People's Republic of the Congo' in A. M. Pappas (ed.) *Law and the Status of the Child*, New York: UNITAR, pp. 183–220.

Thursz, D. and Vigilante, J. L. (eds.) (1975) *Meeting Human Needs: Vol. 1*, London: Sage.

Thursz, D. and Vigilante, J. L. (eds.) (1976) *Meeting Human Needs: Vol. 2*, London: Sage.

Titmuss, R. (1958) *Essays on the Welfare State*, London: Allen & Unwin.

Titmuss, R. (1968) *Commitment to Welfare*, London: Allen & Unwin.

Titmuss, R. (1974) *Social Policy: An Introduction*, London: Allen & Unwin.

Titmuss, R. *et al.* (1961) *Social Policies and Population Growth in Mauritius*, London: Methuen.

Todaro, M. (1979) *Urbanization in Developing Nations: Trends, Prospects and Policies*, New York: Population Council.

Townsend, P. (1979) *Poverty in the United Kingdom*, Harmondsworth: Penguin.

Townsend, P. (1984) *Why Are the Many Poor?*, London: Fabian Society.

Townsend, P. and Davidson, N. (eds.) (1982) *Inequalities in Health: The Black Report*, Harmondsworth: Penguin.

Turner, J. F. C. (1976) *Housing by People*, London: Marion Boyars.

UNICEF (1978) *Inventory of Basic Services to Children in India*, New Delhi: UNICEF.

UNICEF (1982) *The State of the World's Children 1983*, New York.

UNICEF (1983) *The State of the World's Children 1984*, Oxford: Oxford University Press.

UNICEF (1985) 'Universal children's day: a start in community participation during IYY', *Ideas Forum*, 20, 1–12.

UNICEF (1986) *Within Human Reach*, New York.

United Nations (1968) *Proceedings of the International Conference of Ministers Responsible for Social Welfare*, New York.

United Nations (1969) *Proceedings of the International Conference of Ministers Responsible for Social Welfare*, New York.

United Nations (1970) *Social Welfare Planning in the Context of National Development Plans*, New York.

United Nations (1971) 'Social policy and planning in national development', *International Social Development Review* 3, 4–15.

United Nations (1975) *World Housing Survey, 1974*, New York.

United Nations (1978) *The Significance of Rural Housing in Integrated Rural Development*, New York.

United Nations (1979a) *1978 Report of the World Social Situation*, New York.

United Nations (1979) *Social Development and the International Development Strategy*, New York.

United Nations (1980) *The World Population Situation in 1979*, New York.

United Nations (1984) *Demographic Yearbook, 1982*, New York.

United Nations (1985) *State of the World's Women Report 1985*, New York.

Vaughan, J. P. *et al.* (1984) 'Implementing primary health care: some problems of creating national programmes', *Tropical Doctor* 14 (3), 108–13.

Venkataswamy, L. and Kabir, A. A. (1979) 'Nutritional rehabilitation centres and village child care centres' in India, Ministry of Social Welfare, *Profile of the Child in India*, Delhi: Ministry of Social Welfare, pp. 280–90.

Wallerstein, I. (1974) *The Modern World System*, New York: Academic Press.

Wallerstein, I. (1980) *The Capitalist World Economy*, Cambridge: Cambridge University Press.

Walsh, J. A. and Warren, K. S. (1979 'Selective primary health care', *New England Journal of Medicine*, 301, 967–74.

Warren, B. (1980) *Imperialism, Pioneer of Capitalism*, London: New Left Books.

Wenger, C. (1984) *The Supportive Network*, London: Allen & Unwin.

Wicker, E. R. (1958) 'Colonial development and welfare, 1929–1957', *Social and Economic Studies*, 7 (4), 170–92.

Wickström, B. (1979) *Cigarette Marketing in the Third World: A Study of Four Countries*, Gothenburg: University of Gothenburg.

Wilensky, H. (1975) *The Welfare State and Equality: Structural and Ideological Roots of Public Expenditures*, Berkeley: University of California Press.

Wilensky, H. and Lebeaux, C. (1965) *Industrial Society and Social Welfare*, New York: Free Press.

Wilensky, P. (1976) *The Delivery of the Health Services of the People's Republic of China*, Ottawa: International Development Research Centre.

Wolfe, M. (1981) *Elusive Development*, Report No. 80.03, New York: UN Research Institute for Social Development.

Wood, C. and Rue, Y. (eds.) (1980) *Health Policies in Developing Countries*, London: Faber & Faber.

World Bank (1975) *Rural Development: Sector Policy Paper*, Washington.

World Bank (1978) *World Development Report, 1978*, Washington.

World Bank (1980) *Health: Sector Policy Paper*, Washington.

World Bank (1980) *World Development Report 1980*, Washington.

World Bank (1982) *World Development Report 1982*, Washington.

World Bank (1984) *World Development Report 1984*, Washington.

World Health Organisation (1978) *Report of the International Conference on Primary Health Care, Alma Ata, USSR, 6–12 September, 1978*, Geneva.

World Health Organisation (1979) *Controlling the Smoking Epidemic*, Technical Report Series No. 636, Geneva.

World Health Organisation (1980) *Problems Related to Alcohol Consumption*, Geneva.

World Health Organisation (1981a) *Development of Indicators for Monitoring Progress Towards Health for all by the Year 2000*, Geneva.

World Health Organisation (1981b) *Global Strategy for Health for All by the Year 2000*, Geneva.

World Health Organisation (1981c) *The Role of the Health Sector in Food and Nutrition*, Geneva.

World Health Organisation (1982a) *Sixth Report on the World Health Situation*, Geneva.

World Health Organisation (1982b) *The Use of Essential Drugs*, Geneva.

World Health Organisation (1983a) *Programme for Diarrhoea Control: Third Programme Report 1981–1982*, Geneva.

World Health Organisation (1983b) *The Management of Diarrhoea and Use of Oral Rehydration Therapy*, Geneva.

World Health Organisation (1983c) *New Approaches to Health Education in Primary Health Care*, Geneva.

Worsley, P. (1984) *The Three Worlds: Culture and Development*, London: Weidenfield and Nicolson.

Wright Mills, C. (1970) *The Sociological Imagination*, Harmondsworth: Penguin.

Young, K. *et al.* (1980) *Of Marriage and the Market*, London: CSE Books.

Name Index

Subject Index

226   *Subject Index*